SpringerBriefs in Law

SpringerBriefs present concise summaries of cutting-edge research and practical applications across a wide spectrum of fields. Featuring compact volumes of 50 to 125 pages, the series covers a range of content from professional to academic. Typical topics might include:

- A timely report of state-of-the art analytical techniques
- A bridge between new research results, as published in journal articles, and a contextual literature review
- A snapshot of a hot or emerging topic
- A presentation of core concepts that students must understand in order to make independent contributions

SpringerBriefs in Law showcase emerging theory, empirical research, and practical application in Law from a global author community.

SpringerBriefs are characterized by fast, global electronic dissemination, standard publishing contracts, standardized manuscript preparation and formatting guidelines, and expedited production schedules.

More information about this series at http://www.springer.com/series/10164

Charles Foster · Jonathan Herring

Identity, Personhood and the Law

 Springer

Charles Foster
Green Templeton College
University of Oxford
Oxford
UK

Jonathan Herring
Exeter College
University of Oxford
Oxford
UK

ISSN 2192-855X   ISSN 2192-8568   (electronic)
SpringerBriefs in Law
ISBN 978-3-319-53458-9   ISBN 978-3-319-53459-6   (eBook)
DOI 10.1007/978-3-319-53459-6

Library of Congress Control Number: 2017933551

This Springer imprint is published by Springer Nature
The registered company is Springer International Publishing AG
The registered company address is: Gewerbestrasse 11, 6330 Cham, Switzerland

Contents

Chapter 1
Introducing Identity, Personhood and Authenticity

Abstract This chapter introduces the ideas of identity, personhood and authenticity. It shows why these concepts are of interest to lawyers by referring to eleven scenarios which raise questions about the concept of identity. They also show how concepts of identity are too often taken for granted and under-explored.

Keywords Identity · Personhood · Anorexia · Advanced decisions · Dyslexia

1.1 Introduction

'To thine own self be true', urged Polonius, inspiring every other popular song. 'Know thyself' advised the Delphic Oracle. A Google search for 'personal authenticity' produced nearly 46 million results. 'She's not herself today', we say, if someone is ill or acting out of character (whatever that means). 'She's more herself now' we'll say next day, implying that the notion of 'being oneself' isn't an all or nothing thing.

There's a generally held presumption that we can speak meaningfully about a core within each individual: an essence. Circumstances or disease can alter either the core or the manifestation of the core. Medicine, or TLC, or meditation restores the core or allows it to show itself again. Not only is there a consensus that there is a core: it seems to be widely assumed that there is, in principle, no great difficulty about identifying the core: about saying when someone is not being true to 'herself'.

It sounds suspiciously as if most of us think that humans have discrete souls.

These popular presumptions are embodied in the law. There are statutory registers—such as the registers of births, deaths and marriages, which assume (with a small number of caveats) that if someone was born alive and named John Smith, then John Smith he will remain until his dying day. The law assumes that there is no difficulty in principle about identifying the entity called John Smith. Someone might be born Mary Brown, marry John Smith and start being called Mary Smith, but the register makes it clear that Mary Brown is the same person as Mary Smith.

© The Author(s) 2017
C. Foster and J. Herring, *Identity, Personhood and the Law*,
SpringerBriefs in Law, DOI 10.1007/978-3-319-53459-6_1

The law assumes that there is no difficulty about identifying the parties to contracts. Just as in the registers, the John Smith who entered the contract is assumed to be the John Smith who will, years later, be living with the consequences of the contract. To be sure, there's the notion of incapacity to enter a contract—but that is itself an assertion of belief in John Smith's essential core. If the core is affected by drink or disease the contract may be void or voidable. It's the core that is the real legal personality. Indeed the ubiquity and central importance of the expression 'legal personality' is enlightening. The English law is posited on the assumption that we have souls.

The law deals in the familiar, popular way with the idea of incapacity. The Mental Capacity Act 2005s. 1 states, inter alia:

(1) ....
(2) *A person must be assumed to have capacity unless it is established that he lacks capacity.*
(3) *A person is not to be treated as unable to make a decision unless all practicable steps to help him to do so have been taken without success.*
(4) *A person is not to be treated as unable to make a decision merely because he makes an unwise decision.*
(5) *An act done, or decision made, under this Act for or on behalf of a person who lacks capacity must be done, or made, in his best interests.*
(6) *Before the act is done, or the decision is made, regard must be had to whether the purpose for which it is needed can be as effectively achieved in a way that is less restrictive of the person's rights and freedom of action.*

In all of this, it is assumed that there is no difficulty in identifying the 'person'. If that person 'lacks capacity', they are not themselves, or at least cannot act for themselves. Accordingly there is nothing offensive about acting on 'their' behalf. And note what beneficence entails: acting in the 'best interests' of that clearly identifiable person. Even, as we will see, where the biological reality is that that person has ceased to exist.

Section 2(1) continues:

> For the purposes of this Act, a person lacks capacity in relation to a matter if at the material time he is unable to make a decision for himself in relation to the matter because of an impairment of, or a disturbance in the functioning of, the mind or brain.

The draftsman of that subsection did not have the doubts that gnaw at most philosophers and neuroscientists about the absoluteness of mind-body duality. The subsection draws a neat line between personhood and body. A patient can have an impairment of her mind or brain, and yet still persist as a legal entity.

It gets worse. Section 26(1) provides that where a patient has made an advance decision which is valid, and applicable to a treatment, '*the decision has effect as if he had made it, and had had capacity to make it, at the time when the question arises whether the treatment should be carried out or continued.*'

That is: assuming the validity and applicability of an advance directive (neither of which notions, in the statute itself, appear to turn on any question of identity or personhood) an advance directive executed by John Smith in a time of health and sound mind (John Smith's 'true self': we'll call him John Smith A) could have the effect of denying life-sustaining treatment to a second being ('John Smith B') who is only related to John Smith B because 'he' happens to occupy a body composed of some of the same cells as comprised the body of John Smith A. This shows a very dogmatic adherence to the doctrine of a core personality.

The same doctrine seems to underpin most conceptions of the duties of clinicians. There is assumed to be a 'normal' me. The duty of a doctor is to restore normality. A psychiatrist who helped pharmacologically to perpetuate a schizoid episode could expect a rough ride before his professional regulatory body. Imagine that you summon a plumber to mend a broken tap. He looks at the taps, shrugs his shoulders, and says: 'I'm not going to fix that. The tap is simply different from the way it was before. Live with it.' You wouldn't think that the plumber was doing his job right. We see humans like taps.

There is a vast and complex literature on the subjects of identity, personhood and authenticity. We outline the main accounts in the following chapters, and say here only that few leading thinkers have thought that the problems are as straightforward as, by and large, the lawyers seem to think that they are.

In a previous book (Foster and Herring 2015) we sketched out an essentially communitarian model of the person. We contended there that the boundaries of each of us are porous and fluid, and that they can only be defined by reference to the other bodies that come into contact with them. Our shape, in other words, is a function of the pressure of others. We maintain that this is correct, and that only by reflecting the place of each individual in the social nexus of which she is a part is it possible to say with sufficient clarity who an individual is and what rights, duties and other legal characteristics she should have. It's not just that it is undesirable on policy grounds to treat people as islands; it's biologically and sociologically ludicrous to do so. We will have better laws if they do not make ludicrous assumptions.

A word about definitions. Three words appear frequently in this book: identity, personhood, and authenticity. *Identity* relates to that which makes anything (or anybody) distinct from anything or anybody else. Most people would say that it is obvious that the identity of John Smith is distinct from that of Mary Jones. As will appear, we do not think that this is at all obvious. *Personhood* is often, but not necessarily, related to identity. It is commonly assumed that John Smith's identity is different from that of Mary Jones because John Smith is a person (or has the attribute of personhood) and that he is a different person from the person that Mary Jones is— or that his personhood attributes differ from the personhood attributes of Mary Jones. It seems clear enough that identity and personhood are not necessarily connected. A brick and a piece of basalt are distinct: they are not identical. Yet most would not say that they were persons, or had attributes of personhood. In this brick/basalt example we can see that personhood has moral corollaries. We expect things of John Smith and Mary Jones, are inhibited from doing things to them, and assume obligations to them, on the grounds that they are persons. We have none or few of the same expectations, inhibitions or obligations in relation to the brick and the basalt. Personhood, then, connotes moral status. Whether it *is* moral status is a question which we can leave for the moment. We shall be looking at it in Chap. 2.

We use the word *self* as Jung used it. He distinguished between *self* and *ego*. The self, for him, is an amalgam of the conscious and the unconscious, moulded by time and experience. The ego is a brash, brassy suburb of the conscious self: not the sort of place you'd expect to have a theatre or a reading group.

We take *authenticity* to indicate acting in accordance with ones 'true self'. It is, then dependent on the existence of a 'true self', and it will only be possible to say whether someone is acting authentically if it is possible to identify the characteristics of this 'true self' with which the action being examined is being compared.

Authenticity and personhood are connected, and not just because personhood and identity are connected. Presumably is brick is always authentically brick-ish: it is incapable of acting in a way inconsistent with its nature as a brick. But since personhood connotes moral responsibility on the part of the person, for that person to be authentic will entail acting in accordance with the distinctively moral personality of the person. This might not be, objectively, a good thing. An intrinsically evil person will not be acting authentically if he acts in a good way. Accordingly authenticity in itself is not necessarily to be encouraged.

We now illustrate the ideas above by reference to some examples. None of these examples is fanciful. Most of them pose very difficult ethical and legal conundrums, and we have selected them precisely because of their difficulty. We will return to each of them at the end of the book, explaining how, applying the thesis articulated in the body of the book, each of these problems should be solved. But for the moment, having set out each example, we simply indicate, without attempting any resolution, how the issues of identity, personhood and authenticity are engaged, and what our intuitions suggest. In succeeding chapters we look critically at those intuitions through a number of philosophical lenses.

1.2 Deep Brain Stimulation ('DBS'): Conversion to the Music of Johnny Cash

DBS is used in the treatment of several debilitating conditions. It has proved very successful—particularly in the treatment of Parkinson's disease. It involves implanting electrodes in the brain and passing current through them. Sometimes it can change the patient in strange ways.

While undergoing DBS for Obsessive Compulsive Disorder, a patient (we'll call him Ted) heard Johnny Cash on the radio. He had previously shown no interest in Johnny Cash, but now became a fanatic. He bought all of Cash's CDs and DVDs, and said that while listening to Cash he had a 'new sense of self-confidence and felt as if he was the hero of a film.' Both the confidence and the passion for Johnny Cash ebbed when the DBS device was switched off.

1.3 Deep Brain Stimulation ('DBS'): Loss of Inhibitions

A female patient (we'll call her Jane) while undergoing DBS for Parkinson's disease 'lost all social inhibitions, was in love with two neurologists, and tried to kiss and embrace people.' Previously she had been in a monogamous relationship for many years and avoided any intimate contact with anyone other than her partner.

The issues

Most of us will feel uneasy about what has happened to both of these patients, although most will agree that the side-effects of the DBS are probably a price worth paying for treatment of the underlying conditions.

Our uneasiness denotes an instinctive adoption of some sort of belief that there is a core identity, and that this identity is best evidenced by psychological continuity (manifested in what we would probably call 'authentic' behavior—behavior consistent with the type of personality we have already shown ourselves to have). Both of the patients in the examples, being adults, have a track record: we judge the type of person that they are by reference to that track record. Consistency with the track record reassures us that nothing untoward has happened: deviation from it raises a suspicion of pathology.

We know, though, that even conservative adults can change their minds about things. Mid-life crises are well known—although the use of the pejorative word 'crisis' perhaps indicates an intrinsic suspicion of any change. What concerns us in the examples is, in the case of both examples, the fact that the change has been induced by an extrinsic agent (the DBS). But is it really extrinsic? Each patient can say no to the DBS, which would stop the Cash addiction and the disinhibition. By saying yes to the DBS (albeit under the medical duress of needing it to relieve the underlying conditions), are they not inviting the side-effects in exactly the same way as they might autonomously choose to manifest the promptings of a mid-life crisis by going out and buying an absurdly fast car? Is it not irrational to separate our characters from all the circumstances, biological, pharmacological, political, sociological and otherwise, that impinge on them and shape them? Few if any of the decisions we make, supposedly autonomously, have their roots only in our own brains. There is no such thing as a 'self-made man': we are all genetically, emotionally and intellectually derivative, and there is no difference in principle between a shaping force which we attribute to our own volition and one over which we have no control at all. And even if there were a difference in principle, there would be no way in practice of distinguishing between the two types of shaping forces.

Before his DBS, Ted had no doubt encountered the music of Johnny Cash. That he had not, without DBS, acquired his passion for Cash (and the fact that the passion receded when the DBS was switched off) indicates that the 'original', 'natural', and perhaps 'authentic' Ted did not and never would have liked Johnny Cash.

Our inevitable appeal to *naturalness* is revealing, but troublesome. It underlines our belief in a core identity, and suggests that we think that the most important elements of that identity are intrinsic—given by birth or genetics, or perhaps by very early childhood—rather than by anything that has happened in later life. It indicates an atavistic belief in a sort of determinism. Yet if most holders of that belief are interrogated they would admit exceptions. Religious conversion is the obvious one. One can, most would admit, modify identity by becoming adherent to a new creed, although there is often a reluctance to acknowledge that the conversion has changed the core. Religious converts are often said to be 'still the same underneath', or compelled to change by a sort of psychological duress. Disease or catastrophic injury are sometimes said to effect a change in the core identity: we look expressly at some examples below.

How does the conversion to Johnny Cash fare in the light of these intuitions? There is nothing natural about the insertion into Ted's brain of the electrodes used for DBS, but the OCD for which the DBS was performed is probably best regarded as a natural phenomenon. Yet although a natural phenomenon is the cause of the unnatural one, it is hard to escape from the conclusion that the change is itself an essentially unnatural one—and is undesirable on that ground.

Note that we have reached this conclusion without looking seriously at whether the change to Ted really is a change to the core 'him'. It is, at this point in the discussion, simply a change of unassessed magnitude or significance. From which we can conclude only that we are, naturally, conservative naturalists.

We will tend to conclude moral and legal debates about whether Ted should have his DBS simply by balancing the apparent noxiousness of unnatural change against the benefits—in Ted's case the mitigation of his OCD.

On the facts of Ted's case this is excusable, simply because even if the DBS changes Ted's core identity, the effect is, on any view, minor. But it is worthwhile honing, using the stone of Ted's case, the tools that we will need to use in cases where the issue of identity cannot be so lazily sidestepped.

We are naturally laissez faire about the change in Ted for, we suggest, three main reasons. The first is that the change is reversible. The second is that it changes only what can be classified as a mere preference. And the third is that the change appears to have no ethical corollaries.

Now contrast Ted's case with Jane's. We are likely to be far less tolerant of the DBS there—particularly if the change it effects is not reversible. And we can see that our instinctual reactions follow the same pattern as they did in Ted's case. Her disinhibition is more than a mere preference for people whom before the DBS she would have ignored. We assume that it wells up from a deeper place than the decision to buy Johnny Cash CDs, and in any event it is more repercussive and has some definite moral colour: her previous relationships (conceived at a time when her core self was uncontaminated by the DBS) will necessarily be affected by her flirtatiousness and her new attachments. And others too (for instance the neurologists) will be affected. Unless Ted beggars himself, no one apart from him and music retailers will be affected by his pathological love for Johnny Cash.

Our toleration of changes to the core identity if there is a therapeutic benefit (e.g. by abatement of OCD or Parkinson's disease) is also revealing. It would seem to suggest that we regard the conditions for which DBS is indicated as themselves interfering with core identity. Our analysis in Ted's case goes: 'OCD interferes with Ted's ability to be himself. Real Ted is Ted minus his OCD.' That is easier to understand in Ted's case than in Jane's, because Parkinson's does not directly affect the personality. But in excusing the DBS in her case, we are really saying: 'The real Jane is a mind-body-spirit unity. Anything that affects her body as dramatically as Parkinson's will necessarily affect the other elements of her—which we classify as part of the 'core' Jane.'

We can conclude from this survey of the two DBS problems:

- That our intuitions insist that there is a core identity
- That core identity is primarily valued as a source of values—and particularly ethical stances. If the core identity is the same as 'moral status', it might almost be said that moral status primarily connotes moral acting
- Consistency with previous moral stances is perceived as good—provided that the previous moral stance is basically good
- We tend to assume that the core identity is a bequest from birth/genetics/very early childhood, and that subsequent events are, with a few exceptions, unlikely to change it much
- Natural interferences with core identity are less resented than unnatural identity: indeed they seem to be more readily accepted as producing genuine change in core identity than unnatural interferences
- Interferences with core identity will be more readily accepted if they are reversible
- Interferences with 'merely' physical parts of a person may, if they are sufficiently serious, be regarded as affecting the core identity. (We will suggest later that this is particularly likely to be the case if the physical detriment affects the ability of the patient to enter into relationships.)

1.4   Anorexia Nervosa

A team of psychiatrists conducted an interview with a patient suffering (and yes, we know both 'patient' and 'suffering' are pejorative words in this context) from Anorexia Nervosa. It went like this:

'Interviewer: If your anorexia nervosa magically disappeared, what would be different from right now?
Participant: Everything. My personality would be different.
Interviewer: Really!
Participant: It's been, I know it's been such a big part of me, and—I don't think you can ever get rid of it, or the feelings, you always have a bit—in you [...]
Interviewer: Let's say you've got to this point, and someone said they could wave a magic wand and there wouldn't be anorexia any more.
Participant: I couldn't.

Interviewer: You couldn't.
Participant: It's just part of me now.
Interviewer: Right. So it feels like you'd be losing part of you.
Participant: Because it was my identity.'

The issues

We find it hard to know whether or not anorexia nervosa is intrinsic or extrinsic: whether nor not (despite it being deadly) it is a disease, or simply a trait—a way of looking at the world (and particularly that part of the world that consists of the patient's own body and its relationships) that is no different in principle from a religious outlook. We struggle, then, to identify the patient's core identity. Her own statement that 'it's just part of me now' will puzzle us. We want to respect it: our default position is and should be that the patient is the best judge of what constitutes her identity. Yet the word 'now' makes us pause and makes us wonder whether 'it' is an invader—a thing that has assaulted and occupied the patient. Indeed the word 'it' is troubling. It makes us think of demonic possession. A friend of one of the authors, an extremely eminent consultant psychiatrist, not given to mysticism or parabolic expression, said that his own wife's anorexia seemed to him to be like nothing so much as possession.

That the patient sees 'it' as part of her may increase, rather than decrease, our disquiet. It may indicate not that the occupation is welcomed, but simply that it is malignantly complete, involving the will. That might increase our resolve to cure 'it' or exorcise 'it'—to save the patient from that part of herself that is trying to kill 'her'. And there, we note, we have made up our minds after all about what her core identity is and what it is not.

Legal dilemmas about anorexia nervosa typically occur in the context of compulsory treatment—and notably compulsory feeding. We will return in the final chapter to some of the decisions of the courts, and merely note now that when faced with the essentially metaphysical mystery of anorexia, we and the judges tend to rush nervously to reassuring categories that we can understand, however inadequately those categories reflect the complex clinical and human realities. Thus when a patient suffering from anorexia nervosa needs to be fed in order to survive, the analysis tends to be either:

(a) The patient suffers from a mental illness.
(b) Compulsory treatment is justified (in England under the Mental Health Act).

   Or:

(a) The patient lacks capacity to make decisions for herself.
(b) Accordingly a decision can be made on her behalf. The decision must be the decision that is in the patient's best interests.

We observe that in both cases the question of who the patient *is* is conventionally not addressed at all. It is assumed that there is no difficulty about this. In the first case the question of whether anorexia nervosa constitutes a mental illness (which therefore triggers the Mental Health Act remedies) tends to be decided simply by looking in the book containing the list of recognized mental illnesses (a mutating, evolving list) to see if anorexia is included. The boundary between mere traits and mental illness is sometimes acknowledged to be uncertain (for instance in the case of personality disorder), but in the case of anorexia nervosa there is no such uncertainty: the psychiatrists (and the lawyers who take their cue from them) see anorexia nervosa rather like a femoral fracture: you either have it or you don't. And while ones decision not to seek treatment for a femoral fracture may well be respected, a decision not to seek treatment for anorexia nervosa, or to eat when eating is clearly desirable when judged by the criterion of the patient's weight, may well not be.

The conclusion that a patient has a mental illness, or that a decision is made in the best of a patient, requires one to specify the patient. Very often it is simply assumed that the patient is simply her name: 'X has anorexia nervosa'. We think that the complexity of any human being (let alone the complexity of a patient with anorexia nervosa) warrants a more nuanced inquiry into the nature of X than this.

1.5 Body Dysmorphic Disorder

Barry is 22 years old. He believes that his perfectly normal right leg is grotesquely deformed. He is repeatedly assured that it is not. A diagnosis of Body Dysmorphic Disorder ('BDD') is made. Various psychiatric interventions are tried and fail. In despair, Barry contacts an orthopaedic surgeon and begs him to amputate the leg at the hip.

The issues

Suppose, for the sake of argument, that Barry has always—or at least for as long as he can remember—felt this way. If that's right, then perhaps we should begin by assuming that the purpose of medicine is to restore—or preserve—normality insofar as possible, and then move straight on to ask what, in this case, is normal? If we say that it is normal to have two legs, we need to be clear what we're doing. We might be doing one or both of two things. We might be adopting a species-based (or, to be pejorative, species-ist) definition of normality. According to such an account, what is normal is what is usual—or at least within the bell-curve of normality—for members of the species. The objections to such a contention are obvious and well known. Respect for autonomy should demand a very critical look at such an account: the law is, at least in theory, robust in its defence of even life-endangering eccentricity. It would be curious if it were less robust in defending limb-endangering eccentricity. If this is the analysis adopted, the typical caution would be: 'Be very careful that Barry is indeed acting autonomously, rather than under compulsion from a psychiatric condition.' But this is a dangerous caution, because it (usually uncritically) imports the (rebuttable) presumption that a person who has a psychiatric condition that makes him make choices that are regarded as eccentric will not be acting autonomously. In other words it is a caution that has the tendency to bypass the whole inquiry into the question of what constitutes normality.

If this species-based account (or attribute-based account) is not adopted, there is another, closely related possibility, based on what it is assumed is necessary for humans to thrive. It is better for humans, goes this account, to walk on two legs rather than hobble on one. If this is adopted, against Barry's insistence that he will be better off without his right leg, then Barry's view of what constitutes his own thriving will be subjugated to normative (though empirically informed) claims about the nature of thriving.

There are other important but less interesting issues in play too—notably in relation to what it is legitimate for medical professionals to do. Even if we accept the working assumption that medicine's normal business the preservation or restoration of normality, and if we agree that what Barry is asking for is a surgical gift of normality, the circumstances of his request are so bizarre that it might be said that to acquiesce would affect the confidence that patients generally have in the medical profession, to the overall detriment of the community. If that is right, then Barry's desire may have to sacrificed for the greater good.

1.6   Advance Directives

At the age of 50, when she was fit and well, Jean executed an advance directive, compliant with the formalities of the Mental Capacity Act, saying that if she was ever found to have Alzheimer's disease she wanted to forgo all life-sustaining treatment.

She is now 75. Alzheimer's disease was (accurately) diagnosed 2 years ago. She lives in a nursing home, and appears blissfully happy. Before the diagnosis she was a very anxious person. The disease has stripped away a lot of her cerebral cortex, but also all her anxieties. She spends the day watching with huge apparent enjoyment the daytime TV she previously despised, and the evenings laughing and joking with the nurses and the other patients. Everyone who knew her previously comments that there is no apparent continuity between the old Jean and the new Jean. Yes, the body looks the same, but the new Jean seems to retain none of the memories of the old Jean, and certainly has none of the same attitudes or preferences.

Jean gets a chest infection. It would be easy and untraumatic to treat it. The treatment would just be five days of oral antibiotics. But Jean's daughter, who happens to be the sole beneficiary under the will, produces the advance directive and states that it would be an assault if Jean's clinicians gave her the antibiotics.

Jean is plainly incapacitous in the sense that she cannot understand the consequences either of receiving or not receiving the antibiotics. A decision will have to be made for her.

Her doctor proposes to give Jean the medication, saying: 'I have a duty to treat the patient in front of me. That is a patient who plainly wants to live. I owe no duty to a dead woman [the old Jean] who happened to sign a piece of paper twenty-five years ago. Why should that piece of paper be a warrant of execution of a woman who didn't exist at the time the document was signed? I wouldn't be justifying in killing, on the instructions of a woman twenty-five years ago, a baby born today. Why then should I be complicit in Jean's death?'

Before we can identify the issues, some discussion is necessary. We'll call the pre-dementia Jane (who made the advance directive), Jane 1, and the Jane with dementia Jane 2.

A few facts are uncontentious. Their materiality will not be uncontentious. The uncontentious facts are:

(a) The personalities of Jane 1 and Jane 2 are very different.
(b) If Jane 1 still exists, the advance directive would seem to be at least relevant to, if not determinative of, her 'best interests'. Respect for someone's autonomy is plainly pertinent to the issue of best interests (although we contend that there are circumstances in which it might be in someone's best interests to act contrary to their autonomy, even where there can be no question about the identity of the person whose autonomy interests are being truncated or bypassed. We suggest, though, that most—but not all—of such circumstances arise in situations where, although autonomy is being truncated, that subject's autonomy is actually being *respected*).
(c) If Jane 2 can be said to exist, and to be independent (or sufficiently independent) of Jane 1, it is plainly not in Jane 2's best interests for the advance directive to take effect as anticipated by Jane 1.
(d) There is plainly some continuity between Jane 1 and Jane 2. Jane 2's body contains some cells that were also present in Jane 1's body. The number of those cells will diminish over time. Each of the cells in both bodies, however, contains the same DNA. This DNA is not shared with anyone else on the planet. Thus in that sense Jane 1 and Jane 2 are more alike each other than they are like anyone else. The DNA is very important. It gives instructions for the manufacture of the proteins which constitute and regulate the bodies of both Jane 1 and Jane 2. Yet there is no genetic determinism: we are in the epigenetic age. Environment, we know, plays a crucial part in the way that the genes express themselves. Genes are switched on and off by the environment.
    The neurones in Jane 1 and Jane 2's brain do not die and are not replaced in the same way as cells in their other organs. Accordingly, if one takes the view that their 'selves' are more likely to be located in their brains than in other parts of their bodies, or that more of their 'selves' are located in their brains than elsewhere, then the fact that Jane 2's neurones are all or almost all neurones that Jane 1 had will weigh heavily with you in deciding whether Jane 1 and Jane 2 are the same person. But there are three very important things to remember. First: Jane 2, by reason of the Alzheimer's Disease, has lost many of the neurones possessed by Jane 1. Second: it is a fair presumption that if mental

characteristics are determined purely by the physical constitution of the brain, then they are not determined simply by the number of neurones, but by the relationships between neurones. Jane 2 has fewer neurones than Jane 1, but one cannot simply say that the difference between them is the number of neurones. As the number of neurones diminishes in Jane 2 with her advancing Alzheimer's Disease, the remaining neurones relate to each other in ways that would not have occurred in Jane 1. The disease creates a completely new neurological ecosystem—not just a recognizable but diminished Jane 1. And third (a point related to the second): normal brains are plastic. They change all the time. This plasticity consists in the number and nature of the connections between neurones. For the purposes of our Jane 1/Jane 2 case this observation cuts both ways. Everyone's brain changes all the time: I have a different set of neuronal connections this week than I did last, and yet few would describe the essential 'me' as different this week from last. If a substantial amount of brain tissue is lost, as with Alzheimer's Disease, the number and nature of the neuronal connections will be significantly different from that which would have occurred with natural brain evolution. The difference in the scale of the change between Jane 1 and Jane 2 might entail a difference between Jane 1 and Jane 2 that is qualitatively different from that between an undiseased Jane 1 at time x and at time $x +$ (say 10) years. That qualitative difference might (if one subscribes to the Self = Brain view) mean that Jane 1 has a different identity from Jane 2.

(e) Jane 2's relationships will, for better or for worse, have been affected by her Alzheimer's Disease. They are not the same as those of Jane 1.

The issues

(a) Is identity located in the brain?
(b) If not, where is it located?
(c) If identity is not located in the brain, is enough of it located in the brain for significant brain changes to affect it?
(d) Is identity a creature of our relationships?
(e) Are the changes in Jane 2's brain and/or her relationships sufficient to mean that her identity is different from that of Jane 1?
(f) If they are, does that resolve the question of the authority over Jane 2 that Jane 1's advance directive should have? Is the only real question: 'Who is the patient?' Or could it be legitimate on some (and if so what?) grounds for that advance directive nonetheless to determine Jane 2's fate? It might (for instance) be suggested that even if Jane 2's identity is different from Jane 1's, it is so important to respect the expression of Jane 1's autonomy interests in the advance directive that Jane 2 should be sacrificed to ensure that there is no breach in the legal bulwark that protects autonomy. This, we can see, is arguable. Certainly Jane 1 and others in her position gain a great deal of peace of mind (at a time when their minds are working optimally, and need reassurance) from the assumption that their expressed wishes will be respected. Many (perhaps most) people with advanced Alzheimer's disease will not have

as clear an interest in staying alive as Jane 2 appears to have. Perhaps, on balance, and being rigorously utilitarian about it, more suffering would be averted by refusing to admit that the creation of a new identity has any legal consequences. Such policy-based reasoning is common in the law.

1.7 Permanent Vegetative State

A boy, Terence, is crushed in a crowd. The blood supply to his brain is interrupted. He goes into a Permanent Vegetative State. The diagnosis (which is correctly made) means that he will never again have any capacity for any sensation of any kind. He has no pains and no pleasures. His family sit by his bedside for hours every day for years. He has no idea that they are there. He can breathe unaided. He is fed via a nasogastric tube. Eventually his parents say: 'Enough is enough. Terence really died years ago. What's on the bed is just an empty shell. Stop the feeding.'

The issues

(a) Terence is biologically alive. In English law he is alive for all purposes (*Airedale NHS Trust v Bland* [1993] AC 789). But does that really reflect the legal and ethical realities? Presumably it is neither ethically nor legally sufficient for 'the person in that bed over there' to be alive. Aliveness must surely attach to identity: do we not have to be able to say 'Terence is alive' or 'Terence is dead'?

(b) If so, is *Terence* alive? Does not to assert that *he* is entail a belief that identity does not reside, or reside sufficiently, in the brain? Remember the discussion about Jane 1 and Jane 2. The damage to Terence's brain is far more structurally and functionally significant than that to Jane 2's brain. If Terence is still Terence, then where does his identity reside? In all of him? In the parts of his body which remain in the same undamaged state in which they were in when he was unequivocally Terence? In his history? In his network of relationships? (But if so, what should we say about the fact that his relationships are, as were Jane 2's, materially different from those he enjoyed in his previous state?). Or is Terence (and was Terence always?) simply an idea?—an idea which has been changed by medical circumstances but which has, unless and until it is appropriated by lawyers, no real consequences?

(c) As with Jane 1 and Jane 2, are we in danger of resting too much on the notion of identity? Do not all the difficulties and questions we have identified mean that it is unsafe to lean too heavily (or at all?) on it when we have questions of obvious ethical importance? Should we not bypass it completely and instead try to locate principles that do not depend on it? (We return to this question in the final chapter, but will simply say here that we have found it harder than we originally anticipated to find such principles).

1.8   Criminal Liability and Temporary Aberration: Self-induced Intoxication

Jonathan is a gentle, considerate, loving teetotaler. One night, saddened by his book sales, he drinks a bottle of whisky. He becomes enraged, and strangles his wife. In the morning, when he sees what he has done (and although he has no memory at all of the events of the previous night) he is consumed with remorse, and resolves to spend his life trying to atone. He is arrested, charged with murder, and finally convicted of manslaughter on the grounds of diminished responsibility. The psychiatric reports indicate that there is no possibility at all of any repetition of comparable behavior.

The issues

We'll call the gentle, considerate, loving teetotaler Jonathan Normal—or JN for short. We'll call the killer Jonathan Homicide—JH.

(a) Is JN the same as JH?
(b) If JH is not the same as JN, is he sufficiently different to warrant treating JH differently from JN?
(c) Do we need to decide whether JN and JH are the same? Shouldn't the criminal justice system punish acts rather than individuals? Do we need to distinguish, when asking this question, between the substantive law of homicide and the law relating to sentencing for homicide? If *mens rea* is an element of homicide, don't you have to identify the mind that bears the *mens rea*? If so, doesn't that mean coming to a conclusion about whether JH and JN are the same? Or is that a conclusion that is relevant (only?) when sentencing the man in the dock? If it is relevant to sentencing, and there is a real difference between JN and JH, isn't it strange that matters pertaining to JH's sentence are relevant to JN's sentence?
(d) Is it relevant, and if so how, that JN's transformation into JH was effected by an agent extraneous to JN—alcohol? Does that make the transformation ethically/legally different from one effected by a natural change? Is the fact that the alcohol was self-administered relevant—assuming that there really is no risk of repetition?
(e) Is JN's absence of any memory of JH's heinous act relevant, and if so how?

1.9   Criminal Liability and Temporary Aberration: Dissociative Identity Disorder

James suffers from a condition known as Dissociative Identity Disorder, in which several personas appear to cohabit. While one of them (whom we will call Hyde) is dominant, James (if it is indeed him) goes onto the street and bludgeons a passer-by to death. By the time that James is arrested, Hyde has regressed, and has been replaced by the eminently respectable Jekyll. The medical evidence is that Hyde can be pharmacologically killed. James, who has no idea where Hyde was or what Hyde was doing, happily agrees to the death of Hyde.

Issues

(a) Is this case materially different from the case of JN and JH? If so how?
(b) Should James have such complete dominion over Hyde? Could it not be argued that Hyde should have similarly complete dominion over James? If the answer is no, do we say this because we are judging the reality of an identity by reference to the morality of the acts performed by a particular identity, rather than strictly by reference to the evidence about the reality of that identity?

1.10   Suicidal Ideation

Kate is severely depressed. She makes a bolt for the edge of a cliff, but is rugby-tackled by Dave, sectioned, and admitted to a mental hospital. Her depression is treated. Several months later she writes a letter to Dave, thanking him for 'saving' 'her', and saying that at the time she was 'not in [her] right mind.'

Issues

(a) Did Dave rugby tackle the person who wrote him the letter?
(b) Should he have been prosecuted for assault? If so, who should be specified as the complainant?

1.11   Schizophrenia

'I am my brother', asserts Ken, who has been diagnosed with schizophrenia.

Issues

Where do you start in assessing Ken's ethical and legal liability?

1.12   Dyslexia

A 7 year old boy, Jim, is diagnosed with dyslexia.

   'It's a good job we caught it early', said his teacher. 'We'll be able to cure it, more or less. There are all sorts of strategies we can use these days. He'll be near normal by the time we've finished with him.' His parents are horrified.

Issues

Dyslexia, one of the common manifestations of which is difficulty reading and writing, is a rather different way of perceiving the world than the way used by most people.

There are indeed, as the teacher said, strategies that can enable dyslexic people to read and write better. It is not clear what the side-effects of this treatment are. Would it, for instance, cause Jim to lose the holistic view of the world that characterizes many dyslexics—a view which perceives context and connection better than that of non-dyslexics? If it does, would the normalizing of Jim mean the death of Jim?

1.13   An Out of Body Experience

Andy dislocates his shoulder. He goes to the Casualty department of the local hospital, where an attempt is made to relocate it under 'gas and air' (nitrous oxide and air: commonly used for analgesia during childbirth). While this is being done he experiences an 'Out of Body Experience' (commonly abbreviated to 'OBE') in which 'he' seems to float out of his body and look down on it. 'He' can see the clinicians' efforts to put the shoulder back in place, and 'he' is conscious of the intense pain in the shoulder, but he has a curious detachment from this pain: it does not seem to be entirely 'his'. Eventually he passes out. When he comes to, he is his normal self, not aware of any division between his body and any other part of him. The clinicians have, however, not managed to relocate the shoulder.

Issues

OBEs of the sort described by Andy are very common (Foster 2010: 145–166). They present a significant challenge to the notion that brain and Mind are identical; that consciousness is a substance secreted by the brain. Andy's experience squares better with old-fashioned Cartesian dualism than with the dogmas (and they *are* dogmas) of modern mainstream neuroscience (which has tended to shy away from serious consideration of OBEs and near death experiences—on the grounds that they can't be what they seem to be, and/or because the established scientific canons are unassailable if you want to get tenure).

There have been *some* attempts to fit these attempts into the existing neuroscientific pigeonholes. To our eyes, those attempts are unsatisfactory, but the debate is complex and technical and beyond the scope of this book. Assume, for the sake of argument, that the reductionist arguments don't work, and that what Andy appeared to perceive was what there was to be perceived.

Most experiencers of OBEs tend to say that the real—or at least the more real—them is the one up in the air. The language is consistently along the lines of: '*I* looked down at *my* body.' The body is not irrelevant to the 'I': the pain in Andy's shoulder was still regretted by the floating, bodiless Andy: but the concern about the body did not have the immediacy that we normally feel about pain in our own bodies.

The issues, then, are about the most fundamental we can imagine. Do we have an identity (we'll rush to call it a 'soul') which has an existence independent of our body? If so, is the body irrelevant to any questions of identity? Or is there a nexus between our body and this other 'soul' in which our real identity resides? If so, is that nexus affected by things that happen to our body?—and if so, does our identity change with the things that affect our body?

A curiously consistent report, too, is that the disembodied state seemed more real than the embodied one: the embodied one had a relationship—though a distorted one—to the disembodied one. If those reports are reliable, we'll tend to lurch away from Aristotle towards Plato.

There are of course many other questions too, but they are best left to the church, the synagogue, the mosque, and the ascetic's eyrie.

1.14 Midazolam and Memory

Since the clinicians have not managed to sort out Andy's dislocated shoulder using gas and air as analgesia, they have to try something else. They give him a dose of midazolam. This is a sedative but also, importantly, an amnesiac. While Andy is under its influence he can plainly feel pain: he winces and cries out, but can hear and respond obediently to the doctors' instructions. The procedure is successful. When the drug wears off, Andy has absolutely no recollection whatever of the doctors' attempts. The last thing he remembers was the anaesthetist saying that she was about to administer the midazolam.

Issues

Andy seems to have lost about an hour of his life. Yet anyone who was in the room with him would be able to reassure him that he didn't vanish. His body was there, writhing and screaming. His responses to the clinicians' requests were couched in his characteristic language. He could recall facts—for instance his name—and express opinions which were consistent with the Andy that everyone knew before the procedure and will know after it. From all appearances, Andy himself was, in every sense, there on the table. All that has happened is that the post-procedure Andy knows (at least consciously: who knows what a competent psychoanalyst or hypnotist might unearth?). That procedure was apparently something that happened to *Andy,* yet it appears to form no part at all of him. The thing that happened was something that happened both to Andy's body and mind.

An hour of lost memory, when it deals with such a relatively trivial incident as the relocation of a shoulder, is probably not very significant to issues of identity. But it is easy enough to imagine circumstances where memory and identity would seem to be very tightly entangled. Take, for instance, the case of Jimmie G, aged 49, an ex-submariner who was seen by the neurologist Oliver Sacks in 1975.

Jimmie was cheerful and forthcoming. He gave Sacks a detailed account of his childhood and adolescence, about how he was drafted into the navy in 1943, and about his wartime service. Sacks was interested to note that he spoke about his schooldays in the past tense, but his wartime service in the present tense. And his recollection stopped in 1945.

'What year is it now?' asked Sacks.

'Forty-five, man', replied Jimmie. 'What do you mean? We've won the war, FDR's dead, Truman's at the helm. There are great times ahead.'

'How old are you?' asked Sacks. Jimmie paused. He was working it out. 'I guess I'm nineteen, doc', he finally said.

Sacks profoundly regretted what he did next. He gave Jimmie a mirror. 'Tell me what you see', he said. 'Is that a nineteen year old?'

Jimmie looked. He turned white. 'Christ, what's going on? What's happened to me? Is this a nightmare? Am I crazy?'

Sacks tried to calm Jimmie down. He left him looking out of the window.

When Sacks returned a couple of minutes later, Jimmie greeted him as he had done earlier that day. 'Hiya doc! Nice morning! You want to talk to me—do I take this chair here?' He did not remember meeting Sacks a few minutes earlier.

'He is [a] man without a past (or future)', wrote Sacks (1986: Chap. 2) in the medical notes, 'stuck in a constantly changing, meaningless moment....The remainder of the neurological examination is entirely normal. Impression: probably Korsakov's syndrome, due to alcoholic degeneration of the mamillary bodies.'

This is an extreme example. But anyone who gets complacent, thinking that they never have any doubt about where their mind is, might like to meditate, with the psychologist Susan Blackmore (2006: 36), on the question: 'What was I conscious of a moment ago?'

One might say that our memories are *attributes:* perhaps even *mere* attributes—no different in principle from the shape of our chin or the colour of our eyes. If that is right, then it might be argued that our memories are no more constitutive of the 'I' than those other attributes. But that hardly seems right. Some memories seem to go to *what* we are, not just *how* we are. It is true that we are not where we live, but sometimes our environment is so determinative of what we are that the distinction between us and that environment seems to be academic. Who was Jimmie? In 1975 Oliver Sacks saw a man. But whom? Was there any meaningful sense in which *Jimmie* existed in 1975? He (whoever *he* was) seemed not only to inhabit the pre-1945 years, but to *be* the person who had biologically existed in those years.

These issues might seem to be of metaphysical interest only. But consider a situation in which Jimmie, in 1975, is so worried by the political situation in *his* present (1945) that he wants to commit suicide. There is no way of dissuading him from his view of the relevant facts. Assuming that we are in a jurisdiction which gives a right to suicide, should Jimmie be prevented from exercising his right? Who, in other words, is Jimmie? Is the Jimmie who is the subject of the legal deliberations about the exercise of that right: (a) the Jimmie who believes that the exigencies of 1945 are unbearable? Or (b) the Jimmie in 1975—who will never be able to disabuse himself of his belief about those exigencies? Or (c) something else?

References

Blackmore S (2006) Consciousness: a very short introduction. OUP, Oxford
Foster C (2010) Wired for God: the biology of spiritual experience. Hodder, London
Foster C, Herring J (2015) Altruism, welfare and the law. Springer, Heidelberg
Sacks O (1986) The man who mistook his wife for a hat. Picador, London

Chapter 2
Theories of Personhood

Abstract This chapter continues to explore the concept of personhood. It considers the use of the concept in the bioethical literature and provides a critique of the two leading conceptions of personhood: those relying on mental capabilities and those relying on membership of the human species.

Keywords Personhood · Disability · Autonomy · Animals · Species

2.1 Introduction

Many of the major debates in medical law and human rights law boil down to a dispute over personhood. Is a fetus a "person" and so deserving of a right to life? Is there a justification for giving human beings greater rights than other animals? What is the moral status of people with profound mental impairments? But the question is of even greater significance than these questions imply because it goes to the heart of what makes human living good and valuable.

This chapter will start with a brief discussion of the nature of personhood. It will then set out the two most prominent schools of thought on what is core to the nature of personhood: that which emphasises mental capabilities, and that which emphasises species membership. It will be argued that neither of these is satisfactory. In Chap. 3 an alternative concept of personhood will be proposed.

2.2 The Concept of Personhood

For the uninitiated it might be thought that personhood is a reference to a biological concept—meaning a human being. In fact, in the bioethical and philosophical literature it refers to a moral claim: that the being is entitled to have the highest moral status. That means that the definition of personhood raises profound issues about what is of moral value. It is only once we have determined what is morally significant that we can determine who is a person and is therefore a proper object of moral concern. It is not surprising, therefore, that the debates over personhood have been fierce.

It is generally assumed that the term personhood applies to human beings, or at least most of them. The assumption is that there are no entities, or at least none that we know of, who could be of higher moral status than persons. Someone who rescued an artwork before a person from a burning building would be seen as having a made a major moral mistake, even by an ardent art lover (Jaworska 2007). Personhood is, therefore, used to explain why one entity (a person), has an enhanced moral status as compared with another (a non-person). In legal terms the concept of personhood is sometimes used to determine whether a claimant is entitled to rely on certain human rights or other legal claims which are restricted to persons (Griffin 2009). Hence in many western jurisdictions a fetus acquires personhood on birth and is only entitled to human rights at that point.

Personhood is typically seen as being a threshold concept. This means that if a being falls below the threshold it lacks the moral status of personhood, even though it may have some attributes of moral value and have interests deserving of protection. So a conclusion that, for example, a dog is not deserving of the status of a person does not mean the dog has no interests or no moral status: it simply lacks the very high status that is attached to being a person. All those who cross the threshold for being a person are equally entitled to all the claims attached to personhood. No distinction is drawn between the moral status of those who only just cross the threshold and those who undoubtedly cross it.

These aspects of the concept of personhood are tied to the idea that all people are equal. Killing a person is wrong, regardless of their characteristics—e.g. their age, personality or social circumstances (Griffin 2009). Personhood is at the heart of the belief that, to adapt the wording of the American Constitution, "All persons have been created equally". The notion of equality is a central part of the appeal of the concept of personhood. The belief in the inherent value of all persons rejects views that have plagued history: that one group of people is of higher status than another; be that men, white people, Christians, or the nobility.

2.3   Standard Definitions of Personhood

Most of the standard accounts of personhood take a similar approach. They list the factors which are determinative of personhood and use these to ascertain whether a being has or does not have personhood. Even among those who agree on the criteria there is still plenty of scope for debate over the extent to which a capability need be shown, and the response to an entity which has the potential to develop the capacity, but does not currently possess it. The two prominent schools of thought will be now be discussed: those which define the criteria of personhood in terms of mental capacity and those which emphasise the importance of being a member of a species.

2.4 Mental Capabilities and Personhood

One popular school of thought states that various mental capabilities, such as cognition, self-consciousness and practical rationality are key to personhood. The precise formulations of the key criteria differ and might include self-awareness (McMahan 2002), being an entity who can value its own existence (Harris 1985), or being an entity who can experience itself as a being whose life can go better or worse (Singer 1993).

A range of formulations has been proposed. Wasserman et al. (2013) suggest that a typical list might be:

> self-consciousness, awareness of and concern for oneself as a temporally-extended subject; practical rationality, rational agency, or autonomy; moral responsibility; a capacity to recognize other selves and to be motivated to justify one's actions to them; the capacity to be held, and hold others, morally accountable.

Tooley (1983: 44) suggests:

> An organism possesses a serious right to life only if it possesses the concept of a self as a continuing subject of experiences and other mental states, and believes that it is itself such a continuing entity.

Harris (1985: 16–17) deserves the prize for the most concise formulation along these lines:

> Persons are beings capable of valuing their own lives.

It is not difficult to appreciate why these writers put such weight on mental capacities. Their views fit in with some of the prominent values in current thought. For example, modern forms of utilitarianism seek to promote the meeting of preferences and goals, but this assumes that a person has capacity to formulate such goals and preferences. Much contemporary ethical writing emphasises autonomy as a central value, but autonomy is normally associated with the capacity to make decisions for oneself. A table cannot be wronged, as one cannot act against its wishes. Indeed the table cannot have wishes. There can be no interference in its right to autonomy if it cannot formulate what it wants. For Kantians it is autonomy which provides the reason why persons can claim to have high moral value. Jaworska (2010) claims that for Kant it was important that

> … persons are able to live their lives by their own lights: through the use of reason, they can set their own standards, their own values, and then lead their lives according to those self-imposed standards. Persons can live by laws they impose on themselves—they can be autonomous.

Note that for Kant an act has moral value only if it is chosen by the individual. Humans are not (or need not be) driven by brute animal desire or instinct, but can select their own moral principles. It is this that makes human persons worthy of moral respect and value and marks them from other animals. It also explains why we are deserving of special *moral* status. Or so the argument goes.

Supporters of the mental capabilities approach emphasise that cognitive attributes are inherent to the person. This is generally seen as a strength of the claim. These inherent capabilities do not depend on biological or social environments. The prisoner locked in solitary confinement and treated with no regard to their dignity can still can claim personhood because they have self-awareness, understanding and autonomy. If personhood claims did not depend on an individual's intrinsic attributes, such a person's status would be precarious. They may gain or lose it depending on the social environment they are in.

The cognitive abilities approach is very popular, but faces some serious challenges. We shall now examine these.

2.5 Problems with Mental Capabilities Approaches

2.5.1 Capable Non-Human Animals

Some non-human animals might have the kind of capacities for independent thought, self-awareness and the like that are seen as the mark of personhood. Singer (2009) has discussed a gorilla (Koko) who was able to understand over 1000 communications signs. Plenty of other examples could be found. Most supporters of the mental capacity approach will be unconcerned by this. If animals do have these capacities then we should readily accept that those animals deserve the status of personhood. As Rachels (1990: 173) argues: "if we think it is wrong to treat a human in a certain way, because the human has certain characteristics, *and a particular non-human animal also has those characteristics*, then consistency requires that we also object to treating the non-human in that way." Indeed, far from this being a problem for the mental capacities approach, it is a strength. It means that we can treat highly mentally capable animals with the respect they deserve. Unless one thinks that humans have a capacity associated with personhood that no non-human animals have, the objection that only human beings can be persons carries little weight.

2.5.2 The Problem of Equality

The intellectual capacity approach appears to undermine the principle of equality (namely that all human beings are equal) which is central to the appeal of personhood. If what is of moral value are the mental capabilities specified, then inevitably some people will exhibit these to a greater degree than others. Some people have high states of self-awareness, are more rational, or can exercise more richly (or at least more explicitly) autonomous decisions than others. If such qualities are what generate moral value, how can we avoid the conclusion that those people are of higher moral value than others?

One answer to this question is that what is of moral value is the *ability* to engage in these mental activities. On such a view the frequency or extent to which someone exercises these abilities does not matter. John Harris might, therefore, claim that all those who have the capacity to value their existence are persons, whether they spend their time doing little other than contemplating the value of their existence, or whether they rarely, if ever, exercise their capacity to do so. However, if the *ability* to do something is of high moral value, surely *doing* the activity must be even more morally valuable. Nearly everyone has the capacity to be kind and good: not everyone exercises those capacities equally.

A more powerful answer to this dilemma may be more intuitively apparent to lawyers than it is to philosophers. Lawyers are used to the concept of a category, whereby all who fall in the category are deemed equal regardless of the extent to which they qualify. For example the individual awaking with the most dreadful hangover on the morning of their eighteenth birthday is as much an adult for the purposes of the law as the person excitedly reading a telegram from the Queen congratulating them on their one hundredth birthday. So we might say that all those in the category of personhood are equally entitled to the rights and moral status of personhood, whether they have the requisite capabilities in abundance or whether they just scraped through; or indeed whether they simply have the potential to exercise the desired capacity. That was the significance of seeing personhood as a threshold concept, mentioned earlier.

This response is, however, not entirely satisfactory. First: many of the legal categories which adopt the threshold category are to an extent based on a fiction, devised for bureaucratic convenience. For example, a person assessed under the Mental Capacity Act 2005 has mental capacity regardless of the extent to which they passed the capacity test. The law would simply be too complex for physicians to operate if they had to assess precisely the extent to which a person passed the mental capacity test in order to assess their legal rights. We know that really not all those who are deemed to have mental capacity under the Act have equal decision-making abilities, even though the law treats them as if they do. Similarly, on the mental capacities approach, although we might treat all those with sufficient intellectual capacity as persons, we know that *really* they are not all equal. Some have more of the qualities that generate moral value than others. We are therefore upholding equality under personhood as a legal fiction. The fiction might be justified on the basis that we lack the time, sophistication and effort to make a more detailed inquiry.

Now it may be that some people would be happy with a similar approach being taken about moral personhood and agree, saying something along the lines of: "the truth is we are not all equally morally valuable and some of us have higher moral value than others, but it is difficult to tell who they are and so we will treat us all as equally morally valuable for the purposes of the law". We suspect, however, that many people will feel that the commitment to equality is about something deeper than convenience.

This point may be made clearer by reference to an example. In England, those who live in a particular constituency are entitled to vote for a candidate standing in that constituency in an election, whether they are just inside the border or in the centre of the constituency. Similarly they are not entitled to vote for a candidate standing in a neighbouring consistency even though they are but a few feet outside the boundary. This is a good example of the threshold concept. But now try to apply the constituency metaphor to the notion of personhood as a threshold concept. It doesn't work well at all, and its failure is illuminating. First, the criterion (being in the constituency) which generates the right to vote in a particular place is not something that can be done more or less: you are either in it or you are not. That is not so for the mental capacity example discussed above; nor for the mental capacities marking personhood. You can have greater degrees of self-awareness and understandings, and so forth. Second: there is no particular moral worth in being more or less in a constituency, but the capabilities approach clearly regards these attributes as having moral value—and so it is desirable to have these to a greater extent. If it is characteristic X (or the capacity to have characteristic X) that generates moral value, how can it be denied that one should strive to have characteristic X to a greater extent? It seems, therefore, that although supporters of the mental capabilities approach can still claim to support the principle of equality, they are doing so in a formal sense. If pushed they would realise it is a fiction, created for political or pragmatic ends, and does not wholly (or for many purposes sufficiently) reflect reality.

2.5.3   The Mentally Impaired

The third, and perhaps most significant, difficulty with the mental capacity approach is that certain cognitively impaired human beings will lack these attributes, and so cease to be persons (if their impairment is acquired in their lifetime) or never qualify as persons in the first place. Similarly babies and young children will fall outside the requirements for personhood. Indeed its application could mean that we may allocate personhood to a high-functioning chimpanzee, but not to babies or adults with severe cognitive impairment. To many that suggestion is so abhorrent that the argument must be rejected out of hand. Few people would be content to allow the kinds of experiments permitted on primates to be done on cognitively disabled people. Indeed, such is the strength of the intuitive revulsion at the argument, that it is often seen as offensive merely to ask whether cognitively impaired humans are or are not persons (Feder Kittay 2009).

However, there are some philosophers who are perfectly content with that conclusion. The conclusion shows a willingness to move beyond speciesism—the assumption that all human beings are naturally superior to other animals. Their conclusion is important and salutary. It challenges us to articulate carefully what it is about humanity that we regard as being valuable, and to be willing to respect those qualities wherever they are found. Of course, philosophers emphasising self-consciousness and practical rationality would be quick to say that many people with mild or moderate intellectual capacity would certainly have the kind of capacities they see as the markers of personhood. It would only be for the most severely impaired that personhood would be questioned.

Khuse and Singer (1985: 143) have no difficulty in accepting that a child with Down syndrome may be of less value than a "normal child". Discussing whether a Down syndrome child should be given a life-saving operation, they write:

> Even allowing for the more optimistic assessments of the potential of Down's syndrome children, this potential cannot be said to be equal to that of a normal child. The possible benefits of successful surgery in the case of a Down's syndrome child are, therefore, ... less than the possible benefits of similar surgery in a normal child.

The reasoning behind this claim is that all newborns lack the mental capacities for personhood, and so are not persons. The impairments of Down syndrome babies are such that there is a sufficient reason to kill them. Singer (1985: 18–19) has explained that he thinks those who reject these arguments are speciesist (giving an irrational preference to members of one's own species), which he sees as analogous to racism.

Despite the eminence of these authors and the publicity attached to their views, it should be acknowledged that they are very much a minority in academia and perhaps even more so among the general public. But there is no denying the force of their logic. Is there any way for a supporter of the cognitive abilities approach to avoid their unpopular conclusion?

One response is that these views are based on a lack of understanding of the capacities of those with Down Syndrome or other severe mental impairment. The views (the argument goes) *wrongly* assume these people lack the capacities connected with personhood. Those in close relationship with people with Down syndrome and other impairments can perceive far greater levels of intellectual capabilities than outsiders can.

However, this is probably too easy a way out. Even if we accept that many of those labeled as having severe mental impairment do in fact have the required capabilities, it is doubtful that they all do. Unless the requirements for mental capacity are set very low indeed, it is likely some humans would fall outside its boundaries: this seems obviously to be the case, for instance, in anencephaly and correctly diagnosed Permanent Vegetative State. Objectors to the view espoused by Singer and others will oppose an approach to personhood which excludes even the most severely impaired, because that goes against their deeply held intuitions. We think they have good reasons to follow the intuition that those with severe cognitive impairments are people. We explore those reasons in the next section.

2.5.4   What Is the Moral Value of Mental Capacity?

The strongest argument against the mental capacities approach, we suggest, is by way of challenge to the assumption that the possession of mental capabilities is of moral value. Why are rationality or autonomy or valuing one's existence necessarily of moral worth? Chan and Harris (2016: 307) explain:

> Personhood theory attempts a systematic account of the qualities that enable individuals who possess them to lead lives of value. That a life has intrinsic value, by which we mean value to the person whose life it is, is demonstrated by the fact that the individual in question is capable of forming a view about whether they wish the life to continue or not.

Vehmas (1999) claims that such "bio-utilitarians", as he calls them, are intelligentist. They discriminate against those with "less intelligence" than others, with no moral justification. That, he suggests, is as bad as treating people differently on the basis of their race or physical abilities. Some supporters of the mental capabilities approach might reply that the capability being relied on as the criterion of personhood is not intelligence, but rather the capacity to value. This is a fair point, but it does not go to the heart of Vehmas's claim, which is that it is engagement with the world by means of a particular kind of mental processing which is being privileged in the mental capabilities approach.

Vehmas (1999: 114) writes:

> Intelligence is essentially a normative concept, reflecting the concept of what kind of being a human should be; how s/he should think and act, and in this sense it is more normative than a concept referring to a physical state.

He could make the same point about valuing life. He notes, for example, that for centuries very few people could read or write, and those with learning difficulties would not therefore be "identified" because in a different society they could operate as well as most others. It is, in other words, social expectations and requirements that render some "intellectually disabled" and others not. This is, of course, a reflection of the broader social argument in relation to disability, which says that 'disadvantages' resulting from people's bodies (and minds) are a function of social provision (or lack of it) and social expectation, rather than of any natural disadvantage residing in the body/mind itself.

As Vehmas points out, defining personhood in terms of intelligence means making the intellectually disabled "other" and judging them in terms of *our* experience, instead of valuing them in terms of their own experience. We should acknowledge, too, our inadequate understanding of how the brain works and what might be possible in the future with the help of technology, and methodological concerns about the measurement of intellect.

While much of the writing in support of the mental capabilities approach assumes that moral value attaches to intellectual abilities per se, Kant sees cognition as morally relevant because the ability to select the good and to fight against the (merely) animal nature, is what lies at the heart of virtue—and intelligence (or at least cognition) is crucially connected to this ability. Vehmas (1999: 113), however, points out that virtue need not be connected to intelligence:

> positive and virtuous traits of character are often characteristic of individuals with intellectual disabilities as well: honesty, courage, persistence, love, a lack of pretence and other similar virtues which individuals with intellectual disabilities are often more able to embrace than normal individuals due to the lack of intellectual reflection; we normal individuals often prevent our moral virtues from becoming actualised by the practice of our intellectual skills.

Those lacking sophisticated mental capacity can show considerable affection and love. As one parent (quoted in Bradley 1995) states

> Those of us with a Down's Syndrome child (our son, Robert, is almost 24) often wish that all our children had this extraordinary syndrome which defeats anger and malice, replacing them with humor, thoughtfulness and devotion to friends and family.

Further it is often incorrectly assumed that those with "higher cognitive functioning" use this to make decisions. Many of our decisions are a result of emotional reactions, embedded prejudice, and so forth, which have little to do with cognitive function. The exhausted parent changing the nappy in the early morning may be showing considerable love and care, even if "virtually on auto-pilot". The lifeboat team sacrificing their lives for a stranded sailor may be responding instinctively, rather than making a rational, "autonomous" decision to be brave. When making decisions we typically rely on very low levels of information: we certainly have a very limited capacity to foresee the future. It may be more accurate to acknowledge that humans all suffer from profound epistemic limitations.

2.6 Personhood and Membership of the Human Community

The primary view opposing the mental capabilities approach emphasises species membership. It is simply (this alternative view asserts) by virtue of being a human being that we are entitled to prefer the human species. Williams (2006) writing in support of species preference imagines a scenario in which aliens conquer the planet and claim to be superior to humans and so entitled to dominate them. Williams suggests that if any human accepted the aliens' argument we would ask legitimately, 'Whose side are you on?' He claims we are entitled to say: 'We're humans here, we're the ones doing the judging; you can't really expect anything else but a bias or prejudice in favor of human beings.' As Scanlon (1998: 185) asserts,

> the mere fact that a being is 'of human born' provides a strong reason for according it the same status as other humans. This has sometimes been characterized as prejudice, called speciesism. But it is not prejudice to hold that our own relation to these beings gives us reason to accept the requirement that our actions be justifiable to them.

Like the view based on mental capacities this view has its difficulties.

2.7 Problems with the Membership of Human Community Approach

2.7.1 Why Should Membership of the Species Generate a Claim to Being of Special Moral Worth?

McMahan (2008) claims "that there is nothing in or invariably correlated with membership in the human species that can be the basis of our moral equality". Similarly, Singer (1993) is quick to reject the Williams argument based on the analogy with the Martians. He sees speciesism as the same as a racist saying that people of one race should agree with the claim that their race is superior. This, for Singer, is not good enough. You need, he says, to point to some morally relevant characteristics, (such as, he would say, mental capacity), to justify the claim. Otherwise you breach his new "fifth commandment: "Do not discriminate on the basis of species." McGee (2013) has rejected the analogy with racism. Racism, he says, is the product of a false belief or faulty reasoning. A person distinguishing between races on the basis of a true fact (e.g. that a particular race is more prone to a particular medical condition) would not be being racist. The preference for our own species, and especially our own children, is "primal" and based on "instinct". Our care of our own species is "something we just cannot help but do". Not everyone will be convinced by this. The racist might claim that their hatred of a different race is a primal instinct. Also it might be argued that we need more than instinct to justify our moral judgment.

2.7.2 The Definition of Being a Member of a Species

Another difficulty with the argument based on membership of a species is that it requires a definition of what we mean by membership of the species. This is far from straightforward. We might be tempted to refer to certain shapes that human bodies take, but that is likely to work against the interests of those with physical disabilities. It might also mean that a robot shaped like a human would be a human being. So we might be drawn to relying on human genetics and suggesting that human DNA makes us a person. But that approach begs the question of why having a kind of DNA is significant. As Harris (1985: 17) has pointed out, we share 50% of DNA of bananas. Chimpanzee DNA is very similar to human DNA indeed.

In an attempt to define being a member of a human species in a way which explains its special moral significance, one may feel drawn to rely on the kinds of mental ability characteristics we mentioned earlier. But it may then be thought that the species membership criterion reduces to the criterion of possession of a certain set mental abilities. But not so fast.

Kumar (2008) suggests that one can value a member of a species in terms of the "characteristic life-cycle of the species to which the individual belongs". To similar effect, Finnis (1995: 48) contends that "to be a person is to belong to a kind of being characterized by rational (self-conscious, intelligent) nature." This criterion, he believes, provides a way of valuing all human beings, including those who have profound mental impairments. He explains this by saying that there are two ways a human being can claim personhood. even if they lack a rational nature. First, if they have the capacity for rational nature. So, if we accept that (e.g.) rational self-governance generates a higher moral status, we should value a child who has the capacity for that self-governance, and whomever we can expect to develop that capacity deserves the protection associated with personhood. Second, if a person is "internally directed toward the development of such capacity" they deserve value. This indicates that even if a human being with profound impairment lacks the mental capacity or even the capacity to develop it, if their body and mind are *directed* to that capacity they have moral status. The argument can be put this way: We see in the case of a person with mental impairment that "something has gone wrong". That person is not as they should be, and if we could correct the impairment we would. The nature of human beings is to have rational self-governance or higher mental capabilities. Waldron (2015) makes this point well by pointing out that if an ape has an IQ of 60 we are impressed, but if a human person has an IQ of 60 we see that as a tragedy. We can value the human for what they would be had not the tragedy occurred. Here Waldron is drawing on a broadly Aristotelian idea that our species determines our personal blueprint. Humans should not seek to be dog-like or tree-like: they should be human like. However, Waldron appears to assume that rationality (or at least IQ) is a central aspect of being human-like: we will question this later in this chapter.

There are various responses to arguments such as those of Finnis and Waldron. The first is to question why the "internal directing" of the body is sufficient to generate moral worth. Vallentyne (2005) argues that the assessment of moral worth should be based upon an individual's own intrinsic nature, and not on what other members of the species achieve. We would not treat a low quality piece of art as of the same value as a great work of art simply because the former was directed towards the great artistic ends of the latter.

Second, there is a concern that in arguments of this kind a disabled person is being valued not for what they are, but rather for what they could be, and that doing so fails to recognize their inherent worth and undermines equality. One person is valued for their characteristics, but another is valued for the characteristics they might have had had tragedy not struck. Is it possible to hold such a view and still maintain that we value them equally? This view holds that we can imagine a person apart from their disability. If we tried to consider what an "African Mao Tse Tung" would be like, we would come up against the problem that had Mao Tse Tung been born and lived in Africa he would be a very different person. Similarly comparing a Down Syndrome child to a child the particular set of parents would have been had that child not had Down Syndrome is to compare two utterly different—and perhaps unimaginable—beings.

With these arguments in mind, it may be more profitable to talk not in terms of potential, or in terms of a typical human life, but rather in terms of the good work done by the human community as a whole. All members of the human community contribute to it in different ways, and so can claim credit for it. Feder Kittay (2008: 24), for example, asserts that:

> species membership is particularly important to human beings because it means that we partake of a form of life, that is, we share interests, activities, hopes, dreams, fears, forms of sensual and emotional experiences, and ways of knowing the world and other humans, all of which are species-specific, even if culturally differentiated.

She then comments that "such non-individual based considerations [are] part of the rich tapestry in which moral considerations are set."

Mulhall (2002: 20) has developed this point particularly well in a passage worth citing in full:

> The forms of embodied common life open to distinctively human creatures provide the context within which our notion of personhood has the sense it has. These forms are not the practical enactment of a logically prior intellectual hypothesis about capacity-possession that might turn out to be metaphysically ungrounded. In other words, our concept of a person is an outgrowth or aspect of our concept of a human being; and that concept is not merely biological but rather a crystallization of everything we have made of our distinctive species nature. To see another as a human being is to see her as a fellow-creature – another being whose embodiment embeds her in a distinctive form of common life with language and culture, and whose existence constitutes a particular kind of claim on us. We do not strive (when we do strive) to treat human infants and children, the senile and the severely disabled as fully human because we mistakenly attribute capacities to them that they lack, or because we are blind to the merely biological significance of a species boundary. We do it (when we do) because they are fellow human beings, embodied creatures who will come to share, or have already shared, in our common life, or whose inability to do so is a result of the shocks and ills to which all human flesh and blood is heir – because there but for the grace of God go I.

Critics of this view may reply in several ways. One response developed by McMahan (2005), is that those with cognitive impairments do not share in the common life because their impairments mean they lack the abilities needed to do so. In a similar vein, Rachels (1986: 76–7) argues that a severely impaired individual has merely a biological link with other people, but no link to the morally valuable endeavours of human civilization. Further, we can imagine a society which regarded those with severe cognitive impairment as a serious burden on society and shut them off in large institutions—literally "out of sight and out of mind". Would those with severe cognitive impairment cease to have personhood in such a society?

2.8 Conclusion

Our objection to both the standard approaches to defining personhood is that both rest on a particular understanding of an *ideal* person. The standard approaches take the able-bodied independent, rational human as the model on which the approach to personhood is based. The basis of personhood, on such a model, may be said to be the possession of a certain set of capabilities, or the goods that communities of such people typically possess, or the potential or "natural instinct" towards those capabilities. We need to challenge the dependence on such ideal person, or on any of the characteristics supposedly associated with it.

First, we need to recognise that the ideal person at the centre of such models is just that—an ideal. An ideal that few, if any of us, reach. As Fineman (2008) has argued, vulnerability is a 'universal, inevitable, enduring aspect of the human condition.' We are all limited by our bodies in different ways which determine what we can and cannot do. At different points in our lives, our bodies restrict us in different ways. In one sense we are, at birth, profoundly disabled. We are unarguably dependent on others. Even those in 'prime health' are dependent on others. Most of us do not generate our own power or grow our own food. We entrust our lives to pilots, taxi drivers and doctors, and our finances to accountants. We all have limitations: society is willing to make up some, but not all, of the shortfall. The limitations for which society does not account are labeled as disability. The truth is that we all have profound disabilities of different kinds.

Detailed studies of disabled people indicate that despite the 'catastrophe narrative' there is a 'disability paradox'—namely that many disabled people have much happier lives than average. The families of disabled children report being emotionally better off than children with able-bodied children. The incidence of family breakdown is much lower in families with a child with Down syndrome (DS), and there are fewer problems raising DS children. In one leading study only 1 in 20 parents of children reported regretting having a child with DS: the vast majority reported that they loved and were proud of the child (Skotko et al. 2011). Siblings were likely to express strong pride of and love for their DS sibling. Of course raising a child with DS is not all roses, and parents with children with DS are required to spend more time care-giving than other parents, but that may be no bad thing. There may be many explanations for the data from families with a DS child, but whatever the explanation, such studies show that human communities including disabled people flourish, and indeed may flourish more than those without.

Given the wide range of human functioning, there seems no reason to assert a single desirable standard of human functioning for all lives. Feder Kittay (2009: 614) argues in favour of:

> epistemic responsibility: know the subject that you are using to make a philosophical point; epistemic modesty: know what you don't know; humility: resist the arrogant imposition of your own values on others; and accountability: pay attention to the consequences of your philosophizing

Here it may be useful to acknowledge that the world of those with severe intellectual impairments is to some extent a mystery. We must tread carefully in making assumptions about what constitutes a good life. In particular the evidence should make us very slow to conclude that the good in life is a function of mental processes or the capacity for mental processes.

We can find a far better concept of personhood by looking beyond these standard models. That we will do in the next chapter.

References

Bradley A (1995) Why shouldn't women abort disabled fetuses? Living Marxism 82

Chan S, Harris J (2016) Human animals and non-human animals. In: Beauchamp T, Frey R (eds) The Oxford handbook of animal ethics. Oxford University Press, Oxford

Feder Kittay E (2008) The ethics of philosophizing. In: Tessman L (ed) Feminist ethics and social and political philosophy theorizing the non-ideal. Springer, Heidelberg

Feder Kittay E (2009) The personal is philosophical is political: a philosopher and mother of a cognitively disabled person sends notes from the battlefield. Metaphilosophy 40:606–626

Fineman M (2008) The vulnerable subject: anchoring equality in the human condition. Yale J Law Feminism 20:1–71

Finnis J (1995) The fragile case for euthanasia: a reply to John Harris. In: Keown J (ed) Euthanasia examined. Cambridge University Press, Cambridge

Griffin J (2009) On human rights. Oxford University Press, Oxford

Harris J (1985) The value of life. Routledge, Abingdon

Jaworska A (2007) Caring and full moral standing. Ethics 117:460–483

Jaworska A (2010) Caring and full moral standing redux. In: Feder Kittay E, Carlson L (eds) Cognitive disability and its challenge to moral philosophy. Wiley Blackwell, Oxford

Khuse H, Singer P (1985) Should the baby live? The problem of handicapped infants. Oxford University Press, Oxford

Kumar R (2008) Permissible killing and the irrelevance of being human. J Ethics 12:57–76

McGee A (2013) The moral status of babies. J Med Ethics 39:345–349

McMahan J (2002) The ethics of killing. Oxford University Press, Oxford

McMahan J (2005) Our fellow creatures. J Ethics 9:353–374

McMahan J (2008) Challenges to human equality. J Ethics 12:81–104

Mulhall S (2002) Fearful thoughts. London Rev Books 24:18–26

Rachels J (1986) The end of life: euthanasia and morality. Oxford University Press, Oxford

Rachels J (1990) Created from animals: the moral implications of Darwinism. Oxford University Press, Oxford

Scanlon T (1998) What we owe each other. Harvard University Press, Cambridge

Singer P (1985) Animal liberation. Harper Collins, London

Singer P (1993) Practical ethics. Cambridge University Press, Cambridge

Singer P (2009) Speciesism and moral status. Metaphilosophy 40:567–579

Skotko B, Levine S, Goldstein R (2011) Having a son or daughter with down syndrome: perspectives from mothers and fathers. Am J Med Genet 155:2335

Tooley M (1983) Abortion and infanticide. Clarendon Press, Oxford

Vallentyne P (2005) Of mice and men: equality and animals. J Ethics 9:403–409

Vehmas S (1999) Newborn infants and the moral significance of intellectual disabilities. Res Pract Persons Severe Disabil 24:111–119

Waldron J (2015) 'Hard and Heart-Breaking Cases' The Gifford Lectures. http://www.ed.ac.uk/schools-departments/humanities-soc-sci/news-events/lectures/gifford-lectures. Visited 20 Dec 2016

Wasserman D, Asch A, Blustein J, Putnam D (2013) Cognitive disability and moral status. In: The Stanford encyclopaedia of philosophy. http://plato.stanford.edu/archives/fall2013/entries/cognitive-disability/. Accessed 20 Dec 2016

Williams B (2006) The human prejudice. In: Williams B (ed) Philosophy as a humanistic discipline. Princeton University Press, Princeton

Chapter 3
A Relational Account of Personhood

Abstract This chapter presents a relational account of personhood. It argues that what generates moral status is not characteristics or abilities that we have ourselves, but rather our relationships with each other. In particular, relationships of care deserve moral status. It is because we are profoundly vulnerable and interdependent that our relationships are key to our humanity and create moral status.

Keywords Care · Vulnerability · Relationships · Interconnection · Personhood

3.1 Introduction

At the heart of debates over personhood are two profound questions: 'what is the nature of the self?' and 'what characteristics or capacities generate a claim to moral worth or respect?' Our approach is based on an understanding of human nature based on three concepts: the relational self; the vulnerable self; and the interconnected self. We will argue that examination of these concepts makes it apparent that caring relationships are of the highest moral value.

3.2 Relational Self

The human self is profoundly relational (Nedelsky 2014). People are in their very nature interdependent and vulnerable. It follows from this that the basic moral value of humans is not found in their individual capabilities or in their membership of the species, but rather in their relationships. Thus the question "is X a person?" is problematic because we can only conceive of X in the context of their relationships. We can say that X and Y are people if their relationship reveals the moral qualities that we look for in human relationships. But we cannot imagine an isolated person, and assess their capabilities, since such a person does not exist. It is people's relationships, rather than any inherent characteristics of a person, which have moral value and are deserving of special moral status.

Why do we say that we cannot be understood outside the context of our relationships? Because it is through our relationships that our human selves are made (Gergen 2011). We define and understand ourselves in terms of our relationships. Whether as supporter of Stoke City Football Club, a born again Christian, or member of the Marmite fan club, a person understands themselves in connection to others. It is our relationships that give our life meaning and constitute our identity. That is why bereavement and relationship breakdown are two of the greatest sadnesses most people experience, and have such an impact on the self.

The importance of relationship also explains why people doubt that robots could be adequate child carers or carers for others who lack capacity. Even if they were able to do the "tasks of care" they would not be providing human care. There may be situations (e.g. for some people involving intimate washing) where non-human care would be preferable, but that would be because someone did not want human care.

To assert that the self is quintessentially relational is a bold claim: we cannot fully establish it here. However, much current thinking within psychology emphasises the importance of relationality to the concept of the self (Stangellini and Rosfort 2013). In the psychological literature there is widespread acceptance of the notion that three elements of the self can be identified:

> The *individual self* reflects the unique nature of a person and consists of the constellation of aspects (e.g., characteristics, traits, interests, roles, goals, experiences) that differentiate the person from others. The *relational self* reflects interpersonal attachments with close relationship partners and consists of those aspects that are shared with partners and define roles within the relationships. The *collective self* reflects membership in and identification with core social groups and consists of those aspects that are shared with in-group members and differentiate the in-group from relevant out-groups. (Gaertner et al 2012)

It is true that there is a lively debate over quite how these three elements are to be understood and whether one is the primary location of the self. But few would deny that the relational and collective aspects of the self are hugely important. They are central to how we shape and understand goals and how we relate to people we have not met before. Relationship-building has played a significant role in naturalselection. (Foster 2008) Sociology has increasingly recognised the significance of relationality: note the development of Relational Sociology with its understanding that "subjects and objects do not exist in an isolated state, but as complex relational webs in which subjects and objects are defined relationally" (Donati 2015). This is a mainstream sociological theme—not a left-field contention from hysterical communitarians.

3.3   Vulnerable Self

Second, the self is vulnerable (Herring 2016). We are dependent on others. Although we might like to emphasise our self-sufficiency, in fact we need society and other people to enable us to survive. Neal (2012: 200) argues that our universal vulnerability is central to our dignity. She notes that theories of personhood which emphasise the mental capabilities of a person see the essence of the human as a "thinking self". This is a view which goes back to Descartes. It explains why we see the essence of self as separate from the body. However, she argues, we need to acknowledge that the incorporeal understanding of the self has relatively little support today. Once the corporeal self is understood as part of the essence of a being, it become obvious that our bodies depend on co-operation with others and are dependent on the community. The body, by its nature, is constantly open to harms and hurts. We are literally touchable and woundable. But that is not just true of our bodies. Our emotional, psychological and social selves are vulnerable and rely on others too.

For some, to emphasise human vulnerability might be to highlight less desirable characteristics. Should we not aim to get beyond dependency on others, and move to self-sufficiency? We argue not. Vulnerability has many positive features (Herring 2016). It requires us to welcome and be open to our interconnection with others and the wider world. It warns us against puffing ourselves up or judging each other harshly. It encourages co-operation; a looking out for each other. As Neal (2012) writes

> human existence (perhaps uniquely) embodies a union between the fragile/material/finite and the transcendent/sublime/immortal. In valuing us because of, and not in spite of/regardless of our vulnerability, dignity occupies a unique place in the ethical canon; and once we appreciate this, we can begin to ask what distinctive normative contribution "dignity" might bring to a range of ethical and legal contexts.

3.4 The Interconnected Self

The mental capacity approach goes badly wrong because of its understanding of the self. It sees the value of personhood as based on the abilities of the individual. That overlooks the fact that humans depend on community and on others. As Vehmas (1999) puts it:

> non-disabled people tend to forget their own dependence on services, such as the provision of the water that comes out of the tap—an obvious obstacle to their independence. The concept of independence is clearly defined according to society's expectations about what people normally do for themselves and how they do it…. It seems, therefore, reasonable to conclude that people are best described as interdependent since 'people are sometimes autonomous, sometimes dependent, sometimes provid-ing care for those who are dependent'

The mental capacity approach assumes that somehow the capacities people have are theirs and that we can take the credit for our capacities. But the capacities of any person are to a significant extent the result of a communal and relational project. If you must regard my autonomy as something valuable, then credit it to those in relationship with me; with my community and broader society.

Take one example: We could not answer the question, "are you an adequate parent?" The question makes no sense to us. Our parenting is inherently and deeply co-operative with the caring (whether or not we describe is as parenting) of our partners. Our parenting makes no sense without a consideration of our partner's role. Even if you were to ask "are you and your partner adequate parents?" we could only answer in relation to our particular children. We may offer those children—but not others—an adequate level of parenting. Even then we could only really answer the question by reference to the parenting we are able to offer our children in the context of the relationships, community and society which are all involved in parenting.

3.5   The Central Value of Caring Relationships

Once it is understood that we are relational, vulnerable and interconnected, the importance of care becomes apparent. Caring relationships are essential to our survival, our understandings of ourselves, and the things we value. There is not space here to explore fully the elements of caring relationships. Elsewhere one of us has emphasized the following hallmarks of care: meeting needs; relationality; respect; and acceptance of responsibilities (Herring 2013).

So we reach the position that our value lies not in our selves as isolated units but in our caring relationships. As Reinders (2011) puts it:

> Being loved by someone is what matters most in our lives. What we do not often think about, however, is the logic of this statement, and this logic is what I ask you to con- template for a moment. If 'being loved' is the most important thing in our lives, then the most important thing is something we cannot do by ourselves or on our own. Its not a goal we can strive for, it is not something we can achieve. To be loved by someone implies that the most important thing in our lives is something we can only receive as a gift.

We are not committed to a view that only humans can be persons. We do not know if other animals can have (for example) the interest in the emotional well-being of others; a keenness to respond to emotions of others; a degree of empathy; a spontaneous impulse to share with others; a responsiveness to touch of the kind key to being a party to a caring relationships—although it seems very likely in, for instance (and at least) higher primates, elephants and cetaceans (Safina 2015). If other animals do show these abilities then personhood could be granted on the basis of those relationships. Mullin (2011) disagrees. She argues: "Other primates share with us the ability to understand others as animate and goal-directed, but humans have a species unique motivation to "share emotions, experiences, and activities with other persons." Human beings need care, but care from human beings. Animal sanctuaries attempt to release baby animals back to the wild to be raised by members of the same species if possible. Tarzan might have been raised by the wolves with a degree of success, but no one would suggest that adoption agencies should consider wolves as adoptive parents. Gunnarson (2008) writes "When a human holds an infant in his arms or talks to the infant, there often exists a relationship that the infant could have only to a human." Severely disabled infants are dependent on such human caring and relationships for their well-being.

3.6   The Insignificance of Mental Capabilities

We would argue that our relationships are not necessarily based on intellectual interaction. The rush of warmth for the newborn baby is not recognition of a kindred mind. Relationships *can* be marked by intellectual connection, but they need not be: some of their deepest manifestations are not. Many people find sexual relations to be a particularly profound way to express a very deep connection, but sexual relationships need not express such a connection. For many people, but not all, there are points at which words fail, and only a hug will do. This indicates that intellectual interaction is only part of what makes a relationship, and need not be a central part of it. Do people seek in their friends intellectual capacity, or, rather, humour, joy or kindness? It is understandable that an academic, considering what is valuable in life, will highlight academic and intellectual skills. But there is so much more to life than our minds. This is well known to those involved in relationships with people with mental impairment. Feder Kittay's (2009) writing on this is particularly fascinating. She cares for her daughter, Sesha, who is severely disabled. Her powerful essays reveal a struggle to respond intellectually to the arguments of supporters of the mental capacity approach which imply Sesha is not a person. She explains that intellectual capacity is not central to relationships because it is:

> a place in a matrix of relationships embedded in social practices through which the relations acquire meanings. It is by virtue of the meanings that the relationships acquire in social practices that duties are delineated, ways we enter and exit relationships are determined, emotional responses are deemed appropriate, and so forth. A social relation in this sense need not be dependent on ongoing interpersonal relationships between conscious individuals. A parent who has died and with whom one can no longer have any interchange still stands in the social relation of parent to us, calling forth emotions and moral attitudes that are appropriate or inappropriate.

If you are with us thus far, and you agree that relationships of care are the core values of moral value, then cases of children and those lacking capacity are hardly "marginal cases" which it is hard to fit within the model of human value (Carlson 2010). Quite the opposite: their relationships become a paradigmatic illustration of what is good at the heart of personhood.

It might be thought by some that the relationship between people with profound intellectual impairments and their "carers" are not properly relationships because the relationship is all "one way". That is disproved by the literature on caring. There are, in fact, profound ways in which children and those of impaired intellectual capacity care for others. That is why we have talked in terms of *promoting caring relationships*, rather than care. Only a very cerebral understanding of care would fail to appreciate the depth of interaction of which a person lacking capacity is capable. As Feder Kittay (2009) puts it

> We human beings are the sorts of beings we are because we are cared for by other human beings, and the human being's ontological status and corresponding moral status needs to be acknowledged by the larger society that makes possible the work of those who do the

caring required to sustain us. That is what we each require if we are some mother's child,
and we are all some mother's child

From this citation it might be though Feder Kittay is proposing an entirely
passive conception of personhood (X is a person because X is cared for by Y). We
would support a broader reading that requires that the relationship between the two
parties is one marked by the meeting of needs, respect and mutuality. This need not
be an intellectual matter and can include a bodily or emotional appreciation of the
care.

3.7 Problems with the Relational Approach

There are some who object to their value being found in their relationships with
others. Harris (1998) asks: "I can be defined as my father's daughter and my
husband's wife—haven't we been here before?" As she indicates, there is a long
history of patriarchy, restricting women to "feminine roles", commonly defined in
relation to a man. Certainly, as Harris implies, the relational account can be and has
been misused to subsume one person's identity within another's. But that is a
blatant misuse of the theory. We are not claiming that all relationships are of value:
that would be foolish. Clearly many relationships are abusive. It is only relationships of care (in the sense described above), which are of the highest moral value.

Harris develops another point, quoting Brummer's (1983: 235) claim: 'your love
bestows value on me which we would otherwise not have. It does not merely
recognize a value which we already have apart from this recognition'. The impli-
cation of this, she suggests, is that the person who is not loved has no value. In
response, we would emphasize that this demonstrates why we have used the ter-
minology of care, rather than love. While it might be possible to imagine a person
who is not loved by anyone, nearly everyone will be receiving care. We must not
forget the extent to which people rely on a host of care provided by (broadly)
society. The prisoner in solitary confinements may still be cared for by their friends
preparing and working for their release. The hermit may still have relatives who
think of them and are ready to help if the need arises. No one manages to forge a
life which has no caring relationships and does not depend on (for instance) food,
medicine, power or sewers. Even where someone has been held hostage from birth,
this approach shows us the evil done by the kidnapper. The kidnapper has deprived
the victim of what gives life its value: caring relationships.

It might be questioned whether this relational account is compatible with the
principle of equality, mentioned earlier. Does the account not mean that a person
with many caring relationships would be of greater moral value than a person with
few? But this fails to grasp the significance of our approach: we should not consider
the moral value of persons in isolation. We should rather consider the value of
relationships. All caring relationships are of moral value and therefore there is no
valuing of persons per se: it is relationships which generate value.

3.8 Conclusion

In a fascinating record of a conversation between Eva Feder Kittay and Peter Singer, the former (Feder Kittay 2009) says

> Peter, ... you asked me how is Sesha different from a—what did you say—a pig? And [when I shook my head] you said, well, it's a factual question, "put up or shut up." The first thing I have to do when you ask me that question, is I have to get over ... a feeling of nausea. It's not that I'm not able to answer it intellectually, it's that I can't even get to the point emotionally, where I can answer that question.

> ...there is so much to being human. There's the touch, there's the feel, there's the hug, there's the smile, ... there are so many ways of interacting. ... [T]his is why I just reject ... [the] ... idea that you [should] base moral standing on a list of cognitive capacities, or psychological capacities, or any kind of capacities. Because what it is to be human is not a bundle of capacities. It's a way that you are, a way you are in the world, a way you are with another.

This quote raises many of the themes in this article. We expect that Feder Kittay's heartfelt objection to Singer's arguments was based on the fact that, as we have argued, we are defined and constituted by our relationships. Singer was claiming that a central relationship for Feder Kittay was equivalent to that with a pig. But worse, his arguments reveal a narrow perception of what is of value. Eva and Sesha's relationship is marked by care, of a kind where they can respond to each other, meet each other's needs and respect each other. It is personhood at its best.

So what makes you a person? Your intelligence? Your rationality? Your autonomy? Is that all you've got? Are those the things you value in others? Is that what you primarily want for yourself? Or do you rely on membership of the human species: looking like a human or having the right DNA? Is that what generates moral value? We argue that caring relationships generate moral value. In isolation our lives have no great value. In isolation they lack meaning. As the Obuntu people people it "I am, because we are; and since we are, therefore I am" (Mbiti 1969). Our greatest claim to moral value lies not in ourselves, but in relationships of care. Am I a person? By myself, no. Are we people? Yes, if we care. Together we are so much more than we are alone.

References

Brummer V (1983) The model of love. Cambridge University Press, Cambridge

Carlson L (2010) The faces of intellectual disability: philosophical reflections. Indiana University Press, Bloomington

Donati P (2015) Relational sociology. Routledge, Abingdon

Feder Kittay E (2009) The personal is philosophical is political: a philosopher and mother of a cognitively disabled person sends notes from the battlefield. Metaphilosophy 40:606–642

Foster C (2008) The Selfless Gene. Hodder, London

Gaertner G, Sedikides C, Luke M, O'Mara E, Iuzzini J, Jackson L, Cai H, Wu Q (2012) A motivational hierarchy within: primacy of the individual self, relational self, or collective self? J Exp Soc Psychol 48:997–1012

Gergen K (2011) Relational being. Oxford University Press, Oxford

Gunnarson L (2008) The great apes and the severely disabled: moral status and thick evaluative concepts. Ethical Theory Moral Pract 11:305–342

Harris H (1998) Should we say that personhood is relational? Scott J Theol 51:214–222

Herring J (2013) Caring and the law. Hart, Oxford

Herring J (2016) Vulnerable adults and the law. Oxford University Press, Oxford

Mbiti J (1969) African religions and philosophy. East African Educational Publishers, Narobi

Mullin A (2011) Children and the argument from 'marginal' cases. Ethical Theory Moral Pract 14:29–45

Neal M (2012) "Not gods but animals". Human dignity and vulnerable subjecthood. Liverpool LR 33:177–203

Nedelsky J (2014) Law's relations. Oxford University Press, Oxford

Reinders H (2011) The power of inclusion and friendship. J Relig Disabil Health 15:431

Safina C (2015) Beyond words: what animals think and feel. Henry Holt, New York

Stangellini G, Rosfort R (2013) Emotions and personhood. Oxford University Press, Oxford

Vehmas S (1999) Discriminative assumptions of utilitarian bioethics regarding individuals with intellectual disabilities. Disabil Soc 14:37–52

Chapter 4
Identity Theories

Abstract In this chapter we explore the concept of identity. We look at how identity has been understood from historical, philosophical, psychological and biological perspectives. We find none of these satisfying on its own. We rather promote an understanding of the self that integrates bodily, psychological and relational approaches.

Keywords Identity · Philosophy · Self · Parfit · Biology

4.1 Introduction

In Chap. 3 we suggested that personhood was quintessentially relational. The argument was that what generates a special moral status is caring relationships. But what does that argument mean for the issue of identity? If our values lie in our relationships, how are we to make sense of the self? The philosophers have been hard at work on the issue of identity. We will survey their work briefly.

4.2 A Historical Perspective

For most of recorded intellectual history—at least in the West—it has been taken as read that it is possible to talk meaningfully about personal identity.

In the Judaeo-Christian tradition God is in no doubt about his existence and his discreteness. He uses personal pronouns. And if humans are made in his image, they should be able to use personal pronouns too, without constantly and neurotically questioning whether it is appropriate to do so. Adam, therefore, says of Eve: 'This is now bone of my bones and flesh of my flesh ...' (Genesis 2: 23) without apparently wondering whether 'my' is dubious usage. But in the very next verse something occurs that one might have thought would have thrown Adam into ontological crisis: '... a man leaves his father and mother and is united to his wife,

© The Author(s) 2017
C. Foster and J. Herring, *Identity, Personhood and the Law*,
SpringerBriefs in Law, DOI 10.1007/978-3-319-53459-6_4

and they become one flesh.' (Genesis 2: 24) Who is Adam, and who Eve, after this blending?

It does not seem to have precipitated a crisis. The Bible reverts immediately to those personal pronouns. God talks to people in the second person and refers to them in the third person singular.

Yet as the story develops a change does occur. Not in the use of the forms of address, but in the focus of the story. Genesis is the story of individuals. The books that follow are, increasingly, the story of a nation. Individuals matter profoundly, but their individuation takes its shape from their relationship to the nation.

In the New Testament the place and fate of individuals are spelled out dramatically. Individuals only exist fully now, and will only persist eternally, if and insofar as they are grafted into the Body of Christ. The graft does not dilute identity: it enhances and indeed is a condition of it. Even more dramatically in the doctrine of the Trinity, Christianity imagined God *as* a relationship.

The Judaeo-Christian mainstream, then, is vibrantly communitarian. The atomistic individualism of Reformation pietism (from which political libertarianism sprang) was a deviation.

But to insist that one can talk meaningfully about individuals only legitimizes discussion of the notion of identity: it does not prescribe the substance of the conversation. To say that the language of that conversation should be communitarian might hint at some of the substance: it does not end the discussion. The discussion was continued and intensified by (predominantly secular) philosophers. We move in a moment to consider what they have said.

But before we do we need to say a word about non-western traditions.

Buddhism maintains that the idea of the Self is an illusion—and an illusion that is the wellspring of suffering. Hinduism, while tending in the same direction, has a rather more equivocal idea of identity.

These lines about a great, ancient and immensely sophisticated tradition are, we acknowledge, a pastiche. But we cannot say much more, except to point out that for that tradition, although the Self might be the ultimate illusion, everything else is an illusion too, and that freedom consists in knowing fully that all is illusory. While one *can* still construe ethical duties in such a framework, it requires metaphysical work of a very different kind to that required in a tradition where the Self is acknowledged as a real entity. We are simply not qualified to undertake that work. We return, therefore, to the position in the West.

4.3   A Philosophical Perspective

Concern about identity (again in the West) was intimately linked to ethical concerns. Locke (1694) thought that it was necessary to identify a person in order to impose duties, attribute blame, or correctly distribute rights. For him, 'person' was a forensic expression. Personhood, for him, could belong 'only to intelligent agents capable of a law, and happiness, and misery.' Entailed in this account of personhood is intelligent, conscious, agency—and, importantly, consistent recognition of the binding nature of 'a law': those characteristics, in turn, entail psychological continuity. The person at time T2 acknowledges the bindingness of the law at T1 *because* the person is, at least for forensic purposes, the same at time T2 as at T1. Plainly memory, at T2, of T1 will be an important, if not essential, element in this psychological continuity.

Locke (1694) shared with Kant an emphasis on the moral significance of intellect. That involved elevating the brain over the body, which of course involved asserting a distinction, when talking about identity, between intelligence and 'mere' corporeality. For Locke and Kant, in other words, one could not say that person 1 was identical with person 2 merely because the body of person 1 grew into that of person 2.

This distinction proved too simple. It was disputed by many, including Butler (1736) and Thomas Reid (1785). Locke's insistence on the importance of memory as an element of psychological identity, generated an inconsistency, said Reid. Reid told the story of the 'Brave Officer', who, as a forty-year old soldier (P2) in the process of capturing the enemy's flag, remembered stealing apples as a ten year old (P1), and later, as an eighty year old (P3), remembered the capture of the flag, but not the theft of the apples. If Locke were right, said Reid, P3 would have to be identical with P2 but not identical with P1. And yet P2 was identical with P1, as well as being identical with P3. This was plainly nonsense, said Reid, and hence so was Locke's account of identity. Troublesome for Locke's account too, said Reid, was the fact that we change our minds about, inter alia, ethical matters. If ethics and identity were linked, was not an account of identity that depended on ethical consistency flawed? If P1 believed X, and then grew older, 'became' P2 and believed Y, it was surely ludicrous to say either that P1 had no responsibility for X, or that P2 had no moral responsibility for Y. Since they did have responsibility for different positions, Locke would be forced to deny that P1 and P2 were identical. Yet was not that ludicrous too?

There was plainly more work to be done. And it was done. Over the next couple of hundred years these accounts became more sophisticated. They evolved into the (broadly) four categories that dominate the literature today: these are the *psychological account, the biological account, the narrative account and the anthropological account* (Shoemaker 2016). We take issue with this taxonomy. It seems to us that the narrative account is simply a sub-species of the psychological account (borrowing a few traits from the biological account), and that the anthropological account is a straightforward hybrid of the psychological and the biological, sent to school with the narrative.

4.4 A Psychological/Narrative Account of Identity

This is derived from Locke's view. Remember his emphasis on the importance of memory, and the difficulties (exemplified by the 'Brave Officer') entailed in that emphasis. Those difficulties were systematically addressed, and resulted in the following formulation: P1 at time T1 is identical with P2 at time T2 'if and only if [P1] is uniquely psychologically continuous with [P2], where psychological continuity consists in overlapping chains of strong psychological connectedness, itself consisting in significant numbers of direct psychological connections like memories, intentions, beliefs/goals/desires, and similarity of character' (Parfit 1984: 207).

This accords well with our intuitions. But, as we shall see, it has been dealt a bitter blow by Parfit (1984).

A variant is the 'narrative' account. How do I know that a particular attribute or experience is really *mine*? Because, according to this account, it fits with the story that 'I' tell myself about what constitutes myself (Macintyre 1984, 1989; Schectman1996).

This is rhetorically attractive, but it is parasitic on the notion of psychological continuity. It says nothing independent of the psychological account about what constitutes identity: it merely provides a framework into which all the things that have already been identified by the psychological account as essentially constitutive of 'me' can be fitted. Insofar as the psychologically generated version of the self incorporates a statement about the importance of the body to the story, this account seems to borrow from the biological account of identity (see below). It also presupposes that there is an essential 'I' which is the author of the story. So: while we do not doubt the use for many philosophical and legal purposes of the notion of story, it is insufficiently foundational to be the root of identity. It may, however, be the best way of looking at the (secondary, derivative) idea of authenticity. One is 'authentic' if one acts or thinks in a way concordant with the self-authored story.

4.5   The Biological Account of Identity

I wear many hats: I am a father, a husband, an incompetent musician, a human, an academic researcher, an academic teacher, and so on. Yet the huge number of my hats doesn't make me feel embarrassed about using the personal pronoun 'I'. I have had a large number of chronologically succeeding phases: 'I' was once a fetus; then I was a baby; then a young child; and so on. That doesn't make me embarrassed about the personal pronoun either—even though (and this is important when we're considering the adequacy of the psychological continuity model, I have no memory of what it was like to be a fetus or a baby, and it is hard to point to very robust chains of psychological connectedness between me as a baby and me as an adult).

My lack of embarrassment doesn't connote a satisfactory philosophical answer, but it does hint that it might be less problematic to locate my identity primarily in my body than it would to locate it in my psyche or intellect.

Less problematic, perhaps: but problematic nonetheless.

The main problem is a function of the conviction, which we have already noted, between identity and ethics. It is pointed up by a thought experiment in which my brain is transplanted into the decerebrated skull of another (we'll call him 'Steve'), with the result that the other person acquires all my memories and my psychological traits (Olson 1997; De Grazia 2005) (an experiment that anticipates Parfit's 'fission': see below). My skull is now empty, yet a fundamentalist believer in the biological account might believe that my identity continued somehow to reside in me, and that there was no sense in which Steve was me. An assertion that bald is hard to believe. And yet it is clear enough that what my body did matters ethically. For suppose that I, before the transplant, had committed a horrible murder. My hand, not Steve's, wielded the knife. Steve will 'remember' the moment that the knife went in. He will even have the predilections that led to the murder. Yet would it be right to imprison or execute Steve for the murder? Few of us think so. But what about the criminal liability of my decerebrate body, stripped of the capacity for *mens rea*? Should that body be interred in a prison cell, kept artificially alive so that it (I) can repay my debt to society; or given a lethal injection to exact the societal price?

We would be unhappy about making Steve criminally liable. We suggest that this unhappiness indicates (subject to Parfit's objection, to which we return), the following:

1. Identity and ethics are inextricably linked. One cannot accurately attribute moral responsibility without identifying with a sufficient degree of particularity the identity of the person whom one contends is responsible.
2. Some degree of continuity in identity is necessary to make punishment for an unethical act justifiable.
3. Identity is a function of an indivisible unity of psychology/mind and body. Mind-body dualism is fatally challenged by the thought experiments. It follows from this, and from proposition (2), that some consistent mind-body unity is necessary for general moral (and hence legal) responsibility.

One of the important attributes of my body is that it is human. Another is that it is with me throughout the time that I am alive—and therefore for at least some of the time that 'my' story is unrolling. Humans are alive in a human way. It is such considerations that have generated the *anthropological* account of identity (Schlectman 1996, 2014). We do not doubt the insights that this account can give, but we do doubt that in our context—that of practical decision-making in ethics and law—those insights add anything to those that the parent accounts (psychological and biological) can give.

4.6 Parfit: Identity Doesn't Matter

We now look at one important, disconcerting, counterintuitive contention that, if true, would render the whole of this book otiose. This is Derek Parfit's contention that identity simply does not matter for any philosophical—and particularly ethical—purposes.

It is not entirely clear which account of identity Parfit is dismissing. He is certainly a reductionist: he thinks that the facts pertinent to identity (whatever that is) are themselves dependent on facts about the material constituents of the body and the events in which the body participates. And it appears that his main target is the theory that identity consists in psychological continuity—that Person A is identical with Person B if B is psychologically continuous with A, and no one and nothing else has such psychological continuity. We have examined this account above. Variants of this account are certainly the most intuitively popular to laymen; they are also the most popular amongst philosophers. Parfit has therefore chosen a formidable and worthwhile opponent.

His weapon is a powerful thought experiment. He calls it 'fission'.

Imagine that the two halves of my brain are identical, and that each hemisphere could do the job of a single brain. Imagine too that I am one in a set of triplets, and that the brains of both of my brothers have been irreparably damaged. It is surgically possible (we'll say) to transplant one of my cerebral hemispheres into each of my siblings. Each of them will be, therefore, 'psychologically continuous' with me. Each will have all of my memories, my traits, my intentions (and will presumably enact those intentions), my processing power, and so on.

But what about me? If the psychological continuity account of identity is right, both of my siblings would appear to be me. But there's a problem with this: wouldn't that mean that each is identical to the other?—in which case neither my siblings nor I would seem to have any unique identity. Do I survive at all? I presumably can't be both of my siblings: one can't be two. But can I be one of them? If so, which one—since both are identical? Isn't it nonsense to suppose that I have survived at all? My body is mouldering in the grave. And yet someone (in fact some-*two*) which have all the characteristics demanded of identity by the psychological continuity theory, and *doing* bodily precisely what I would have been doing had I not been decomposing, is/are wandering the world. This survival of 'me' in the bodies of the others is for all intents and purposes, says Parfit, the survival of me. Any dissolution of or dilution of or change to my identity therefore simply doesn't matter.

Several variants of this basic contention have evolved to meet various criticisms (Shoemaker 2016). The nuances both of the criticisms and the responses do not matter for present purposes. We simply observe that, despite the force of generic criticisms of thought experiments such as this (see McGee and Foster forthcoming), the thought experiment seems to us to be fatal to the basic 'Psychological Continuity' account.

4.7   Age, Old Age and Identity

In this section we explore some of these discussions in the context of old age. Age as an identifying characteristic is interesting. Those in middle age can be somewhat foggy about their precise age. Toddlers, children, teenagers, and young people tend to know their age exactly, and attach significance, and even pride, to shifts between ages. There is little a younger person finds more annoying than being treated as being younger than "they really are". The relationship between age and identity for older people is complex and is especially revealing.

Old age is commonly portrayed as something that should be fought against and rejected. A youthful old age is the ideal. "You look your age" is not generally thought to be a compliment when addressed to a 90-year old.

The assumption that older people should fight against old age is based on two assumptions. The first is that old age is a time of frailty, dependency, incompetence and wrinkles. The second is that frailty, dependency, incompetence and wrinkles are bad things. We think that both of these assumptions are mistaken, although we cannot explore here all the reasons for why that is so (see Herring 2009, 2016).

Many gerontologists have explored the uneasy tension between the social understanding of old age as a time of loss of capacity and vulnerability, and the fact that many elderly people feel youthful. Such elderly people feel a dissonance between the appearance of their bodies and the way they perceive themselves. They acknowledge that their bodies appear old, and feel that they are expected to perform a role as an "older person", but their inner, youthful self rejects this 'old' identity and role.

In the literature it is suggested that the standard response to the tension between the "youthful self" and the "ageing body" is the use of masks or masquerades, whereby the older person seeks to take on the appearance of a younger person and so escape the negative stereotypes associated with age (Biggs 1997). These masks can range from cosmetic surgery to styles of dress, speech or behaviour. Indeed, there is a substantial market offering a range of products, procedures and life style options which enable a "youthful" old age. Biggs (1997) distinguishes between the use of masks and the concept of masquerade, (a masquerade, he says, is where an older person acts out the role of the younger person.

We reject the proposal that we should understand older people as using a mask or masquerade behind which the real youthful self hides, because it downplays the relational and bodily nature of the self. First, it reinforces the notion of a Cartesian split of body and mind. It appears to reflect an assumption that there is a "real self", a youthful self, which is independent from the actual body, and that in old age the ageing older body is betraying the youthfulness of the younger self. As we have argued, the idea of this split between the self and the body is deeply problematic. The self and the body are closely entwined and it makes no sense to think of a self independently from the body.

Second, the image of the youthful self hiding behind a mask promotes a highly individualised concept of the self—a version in which the true inner self exists, but where a different self is presented to the outside world—so affecting ones relationship with others. We have argued, of course, that in fact ones identity comes to a large extent from ones relationships and interactions with others.

Ageism infects relationships and interactions, and so challenges the very self.

We cannot separate out the real us from the us which forms the basis of our treatment and relationships. To a large extent the self is created by the relational and social contexts in which we live.

4.8   Conclusion

The biological account *simpliciter* and the psychological account *simpliciter* do not work because humans are not simple: because there is no such thing as *mere* embodiment or *mere* cerebration. The psychological and biological accounts fail (and Parfit succeeds in the destructive part of his project) because of their extremity: because they parody the human condition by assuming that it can be described in one way to the exclusion of the other, and because of the necessary distaste that analysts have for any notion that cannot easily be distinguished from another. The discussion of older people demonstrates the strange conclusion that results if identity is seen as merely cerebration or merely embodiment. It also showed the powerful role of relationships and community in shaping identity.

To say (as we do say) that humans are (at least) mind-body unities, will seem to many to be an abandonment of analysis rather than an outcome of analysis. Yet we have reached this conclusion, not only from our own experience of embodiment, cerebration, fatherhood and bereavement, but also by noting the philosophical shortcomings of the principal accounts of identity.

References

Biggs S (1997) Choosing not to be old? Masks, bodies and identity management in later life. Ageing and Soc 17:553–570
Butler J (1736) Of personal identity. In: *The analogy of religion*. Reprinted in Perry J (1975) *Personal identity*. University of California Press, Berkley
De Grazia D (2005) Human identity and bioethics Cambridge University Press, Cambridge
Herring J (2009) Older people in law and society. Oxford University Press, Oxford
Herring J (2016) Vulnerable adults and the law. Oxford University Press, Oxford
Locke J (1694) Of identity and diversity. In: Locke J *Essay concerning human understanding*. Reprinted in Perry J (1975) *Personal identity*. University of California Press, Berkley
Macintyre A (1984) After virtue. University of Notre Dame Press, Notre Dame
Macintyre A (1989) The virtues, the unity of a human life and the concept of a tradition. In: Hauerwas S, Jones LG (eds), (1989) Why Narrative? W.B. Eerdmans, Grand Rapids
McGee A, Foster C (forthcoming) *The use and abuse of intuitions*
Olson E (1997) The human animal: personal identity without psychology. Oxford University Press, Oxford
Parfit D (1984) Reasons and persons. Oxford University Press, Oxford
Reid T (1785) Of memory. In Essays on the intellectual powers of man. Robinson J, London
Schectman M (1996) The constitution of selves. Cornell University Press, Ithaca
Schlectman M (2014) Staying alive: personal identity, practical concerns, and the unity of a life. Oxford University Press, Oxford
Shoemaker D (2016) Personal identity and ethics. In: Zalta E (ed) The stanford encyclopedia of philosophy <https://plato.stanford.edu/archives/win2016/entries/identity-ethics/>

Chapter 5
Summary and Conclusion

Abstract In this chapter we seek to summarise, in eleven principles, our approach to questions of identity and personhood. We then go on to apply these to the scenarios outlined in the first chapter.

Keywords Personhood · Identity · Criminal · Advance decisions · Bodies

5.1 Introduction

In the opening chapter we suggested that questions of identity, personhood and authenticity are at the heart of many legal problems, but are usually either ignored or inadequately treated by the law.

We hope that that chapter illustrated the crucial significance to the law of those questions, and that the subsequent chapters at least hinted that it was possible for the law to address the questions more squarely.

It is easy to criticize the law for not doing very well: it is much harder to say what it should do. It is now time to pick up the specific challenges that we issued to the law in that first chapter, and to say how we think the law should meet them. But before we do so we will draw together the principles which we say should govern situations in which questions of personal identity play a central part.

5.2 Eleven Key Principles

5.2.1 Principle 1

Principle 1: *If you get the facts about human beings wrong, you are unlikely to produce satisfactory legal or ethical solutions to problems involving human beings.*

© The Author(s) 2017
C. Foster and J. Herring, *Identity, Personhood and the Law*,
SpringerBriefs in Law, DOI 10.1007/978-3-319-53459-6_5

This is so trite that it is seldom said, and because it is seldom said, it tends to be ignored. It is an illustration of the computer programmer's maxim: If you put rubbish in, you get rubbish out. In fact many of the supposedly factual inputs to processes of legal reasoning are not facts at all: they are presumptions about the way that humans are, or how humans should behave, or abstractions, a million miles away from the realities. Humans are often perceived by the law as entities whose sole motivation is profit and whose sole justification is economic; or as atomistic entities who have no relationships or no relationships that in any way define what the entity is; or as creatures that are merely the sum of their attributes; or as beings whose overridingly important attribute is self-determination (a formulation unblushingly arrived at without once asking what the 'self' is whose determination is so crucial).

We see facts as epistemically superior to abstractions. Put like that, we do not expect the contention—at least in the context of the law - to be controversial. We acknowledge that a full justification of the contention is more difficult than it sounds, but for present purposes we can get by with the fudge that the law itself purports only to do justice on the facts of the particular cases presented to it.

A lot of what we describe as the law is, it seems to us, 'rubbish out' because there has been rubbish in.

5.2.2 Principle 2

Principle 2: *It is possible to ascertain some facts about human beings of sufficiently general application to justify their use by the law as presumptions.*

This is essentially a matter of observation, but again we think that it will be uncontroversial. It is, anyway, the presumption that the law makes already about humans. And it would be surprising if one could say nothing that is generally true about members of a particular species.

5.2.3 Principle 3

Principle 3: *We are quintessentially relational beings—and hence no satisfactory account of the identity and other related characteristics of any person can be articulated without reference to the biological and social context of that person.*

We play no part in our conception, our gestation or our birth, and although we have an incrementally increasing role in our own lives as we grow up (unless and until disease, incapacity or old age hit us), we remain crucially dependent on others. The thoughts that we say form the architecture of *our* splendidly unique minds were bequeathed by parents, teachers, writers, film-makers, friends and the participants in the conversations on which we've eavesdropped. The very language we use to formulate our thoughts and explain our understandings of the world was given to us through our relationships with those who raised us.

Our environment isn't everything. Our genes too are important, and the combination of genes which each possesses is, unless we have an identical twin, unique to us. But genes are *very* far from being everything. There is, true, some true genetic determinism. If you have the gene for Huntingdon's disease you will get Huntingdon's disease. But such absolute examples are unusual. Genes are switched on and off—often (it is known) by environmental triggers, and often by triggers that are unknown but which may well be environmental (in the sense of being ultimately traceable to something outside the gene-bearer's body). To a first degree of approximation we might say that our health—indeed our biology—is a conversation between genes and environment. And the point about that is that 'our' ability to chair and direct that conversation is distinctly limited. Yes, the entity that I identify as 'myself' can decide (under the influence of friends, magazines, and so on) to eat organic food or meditate each day (both of which may reduce the risk of lethal oncogenes being triggered). But they're no guarantee of success. Indeed there is an absolute guarantee that, however much I desire immortality, I will one day succumb and be eaten by worms—over which, again I have no control. I will then, beyond argument, *be* part of my environment, not merely be influenced by it.

As we argued in Chap. 4, it is our caring relationships which give rise to claims of moral status. In ourselves we are of little moral worth. Our loving, caring and nurturing are what is good.

So, then, what we tend to describe as the solo dance of *our* life turns out to have a company of millions. Our own movements cannot be described except in relation to the movement of others—of which they are both cause and effect. Indeed we put it rather higher than this: we do not exist at all except in relation to others: our self is crucially contingent on and constituted by relationship. A theologian from the Greek Orthodox tradition put it well: 'Egocentricity is the death of true personhood. Each becomes a real person only through entering into relation with other persons, through living for them and in them. There can be no man ....until there are at least two men in communication' (Ware 1979, 34–35).

5.2.4   Principle 4

Principle 4: *Despite our relational nature, the notion of a self is inescapable.*

Humans (along with other higher primates, cetaceans, at least some corvids, and probably a great many other things) are conscious. They have, in other words, subjectivity: a sense of self. And hence a sense of others. That is why relationships matter so much, they both formulate and create an identity and give means to the self and the world around. Humans distinguish between themselves and others. This happens from an early age, and persists, however strong any communitarian sense that may subsequently be developed. They cannot be persuaded—even if they are

Buddhist—that personal pronouns are inappropriate. They fear anything that gets in
the way of the 'I'—whether autonomy-truncating laws, personality-altering dis-
eases or substances, or death (presumably because of uncertainty about whether the
self will survive, or whether the circumstances of any survival of the self will allow
for the self's expression or thriving).

5.2.5 Principle 5

Principle 5: *It does not follow from Principle 4 that the self of a person at a
particular time or in particular circumstances will be the same at a different time or
in other circumstances.*

That there is room for discussion about this is amply shown (even if one ultimately rejects the contention) by, for instance, Derek Parfit's powerful thought
experiment: see Sect. 4.6.

In Chaps. 3 and 4 we saw the role that relationships can play in establishing
identity and moral value. As these relationships change, so too will the self. It is
therefore not only unsurprising that the self changes; it is almost inevitable.

5.2.6 Principle 6

Principle 6: *Even if the self were not a plain physical or metaphysical fact, it would
be essential to posit ethical (and hence legal) rules on a similar or identical notion.*

We accept that to consider questions of personal identity is to get dangerously—
or at least unfashionably—metaphysical, and that this will lead some to try to do
their ethical and legal reasoning without any detailed inquiry into those questions.
We have already indicated that we think such evasion is disreputable, and we note
that those who try to evade questions of personal identity usually do so (particularly
in the law), by asserting that there is no need to undertake an inquiry because the
answer to the question 'Who is the appropriate subject of ethical and legal dis-
course?' is obvious. 'John Smith is John Smith', they say, 'and there's nothing
more to be said about it.' We hope that we have said enough already in this book to
demonstrate, at the very least, that the question 'Who is John Smith?' is worthy of a
great deal of discussion.

We note, too, that the identity-sceptics don't deny the importance of identity for
decision-making. To the contrary: they are all the more certain about their ethical
and legal decisions because they have no doubt about the identity of the subject of
the decision. This demonstrates, we think, that one cannot do satisfactory ethics or
law without identifying the subject. One cannot, in other words, do ethics or law in
the abstract. The lawyers in common law jurisdictions recognize this—according
binding status only to legal decisions that are necessary in order to decide the case

in hand. This is the famous distinction between the (binding) *ratio decidendi* and the non-binding *obiter dicta* (which are, however erudite, not necessary for a decision).

Lawyers insist that duties are important. So they are, but: (a) they exist primarily to protect legal persons; and (b) the notion of a duty is meaningless unless one can identity a person who owes a duty and to whom a duty is owed. The same is true for ethical obligations. If one doesn't have identity, law and ethics simply evaporate.

5.2.7 *Principle 7*

Principle 7: *There is a real and important distinction between the substance of a thing and its attributes—and hence between a human identity and the attributes associated with that identity.*

It has been well understood, at least from the Middle Ages (when the issue arose in relation to the characteristics of the transubstantiated Eucharist) that it is wrong to assert that things are simply bundles of attributes.

Assuming that this understanding is correct, Parfit (and other similar thought-experimenters) can be seen to be less lethal to the idea of personal identity than they may at first seem. All that he and they have done is to show that *attributes* (as opposed to core identity) have (for instance) been transferred (with a brain transplant). The substance of personal identity is beyond the reach of such experiments.

This is not at all to say that such experiments are not important. It can robustly be contended that if the substance of personal identity is so elusive, it must be so mistily metaphysical that it can be dismissed by mainstream lawyers and philosophers in the same way as ghosts are dismissed by mainstream science; or at least that one should make ethical and legal decisions on the basis of the less coy attributes. There is, in any event, an obvious connection between the substance of personal identity and its attributes: the attributes are how the substance engages with the world, and so when one makes decisions which are in and of the world, one should look primarily to the attributes.

While wanting to leave open the question of whether there is indeed a core identity which persists despite the ravages of time or disease, we see the import of that question as primarily theological rather than something which can or should impinge on practical ethical and legal decision-making. We therefore consider that the primary data to be processed when deciding on questions of identity are the attributes. The primary: but not the only. That is an important qualification: it features prominently in our answers to the practical problems that we have set ourselves. The import of the qualification is best illustrated in relation to those practical problems, rather than set out as a statement of principle.

One of the most important attributes of the self is self-determination. As the examples make clear, respect for autonomy is (rightly) at the forefront of the minds of most serious people who consider what should be done in each of those cases. Yet if we formulate 'respect for autonomy' as 'respect for *self*-determination', we immediately see the problem in thinking (as is often done) that respect for autonomy is a free-standing principle that can do all the ethical and legal work. We can't escape from questions of identity.

5.2.8   Principle 8

Principle 8: *Although attributes do not **constitute** the self (being more akin to substances secreted by it), the attributes possessed by a person are clearly related to the self, and may be an important indicator of the identity of a person.*

5.2.9   Principle 9

Principle 9: *The objective of law and ethics is to maximize human thriving.*

Or, to be more exact, to maximize the thriving of individual selves, possessing distinct identities. That thriving is found particularly in the caring relationships between people.

5.2.10   Principle 10

Principle 10: *In order to maximize the thriving of individual selves it is necessary to identify the selves concerned.*

5.2.11   Principle 11

Principle 11: *Attributes, while not constituting the self, may be a useful indicator of the identity of the subject concerned **and** of the relevant thriving interests.*

Sometimes disease or circumstances might alter the identity. Often it will be difficult to say with certainty sufficient for (at least) legal purposes that identity has changed. In such circumstances it may be legitimate to assume that the attributes indicate sufficient about core identity for it to be possible to act. Acting on this basis might look as if one is treating the core identity as a bundle of attributes, but if the analysis has been done correctly this will not be the case.

We go further: it will be quite unusual to endorse an action which denies that an attribute is a genuine emanation from the core self. A practical effect of this is that it can be (*rebuttably*) presumed that to enable the attributes associated with identity to blossom will maximize the thriving of the core self. The caveat about rebuttal is, however, very important. We will see it invoked several times as we consider the cases.

5.3 Application of the Principles

We now turn to the specific examples. We set them out again, for ease of references. We do not reiterate our discussion of the issues raised by each, but simply give our suggested solutions, with brief reasons.

It is important to note that our legal answers may differ from our ethical answers. This should not be surprising. The law has teeth. It often uses them to compel. Compulsion is intrinsically offensive and requires strenuous justification. Ethics, however (except when it is hardened into quasi-law, for instance in a regulatory tribunal that enforces codes of professional conduct) has no teeth: it is only persuasive. There will therefore be many situations where a course of conduct may be ethically praiseworthy, but should not be mandated by the law; or ethically dubious, but should not be proscribed by the law. The justification that should be required before legal intervention is triggered may be made strenuous in a number of ways. There may, for instance, be an onerous burden of proof required before the law is entitled to intervene. The divergence between some of our ethical and some of our legal answers is due to issues of burden (and standard) of proof. The questions we have posed raise profound and profoundly mysterious issues. Rarely is there any certainty. Often we are ourselves agnostic about a foundational element (and when we are we will admit it). That agnosticism is sometimes translated into practice through the medium of the burden/standard of proof.

For some of the problems posed we agree on the answer. On others we disagree— usually only slightly. Where we differ, our respective views are indicated by our initials.

5.3.1 *Deep Brain Stimulation ('DBS'): Conversion to the Music of Johnny Cash*

While undergoing DBS for Obsessive Compulsive Disorder, a patient (we'll call him Ted) heard Johnny Cash on the radio. He had previously shown no interest in Johnny Cash, but now became a fanatic. He bought all of Cash's CDs and DVDs, and said that while listening to Cash he had a 'new sense of self-confidence and felt as if he was the hero of a film.' Both the confidence and the passion for Johnny Cash ebbed when the DBS device was switched off.

Our answer

Assuming that we are asked to adjudicate as to the propriety of the DBS in the light of that issue, we have no hesitation in saying that the DBS is justified. We are not completely convinced that there is a real alteration of identity here. The DBS changes some characteristics, yes, but we are not persuaded that the magnitude of those changes, and their significance to Ted's whole constitution, are so great that they can be said to change the core Ted. We therefore admit that we adopt the popular, intuitive view that we can (and must) talk meaningfully about a core identity—which is not simply a bundle of attributes. We come later to the question of whether that identity can be lost. But it is not lost in circumstances like Ted's. It is unlikely that any of his family or friends will treat him any differently as a result of his new-found love of Cash.

Had we concluded that the DBS did effect a change in the core identity, we would still have considered that it was justified, because we would categorise the Obsessive Compulsive Disorder as a more significant identity-transforming condition than the condition induced by the DBS. Accordingly, since we regard identity as important, and the DBS preserves more identity than it ablates, it is both ethically and legally justified.

5.3.2 Deep Brain Stimulation ('DBS'): Loss of Inhibitions

A female patient (we'll call her Jane) while undergoing DBS for Parkinson's disease 'lost all social inhibitions, was in love with two neurologists, and tried to kiss and embrace people.' Previously she had been in a monogamous relationship for many years and avoided any intimate contact with anyone other than her partner.

Our answer

Identity is more squarely in play here than in Ted's DBS case. We say this because we see core identity as primarily a creature of relationships. Jane's loss of inhibition directly affects her (self-defining) relationships.

This is not to say that every character trait that impinges on another individual will necessarily form a crucial element of the core self. Indeed we can think of few character traits that do not—at least potentially—impinge on others. We have already made clear our view that mere attributes (which may include character traits) are to be distinguished (either alone or in combination) from identity. Identity secretes attributes: we should not confuse the secretor and the secreted. Nor is this to say the fact that another is affected by a trait should mean that a deleterious effect of that trait on the other justifies the suppression of that trait: many exercises of autonomy will affect the autonomy of others. Such issues are to be dealt with legally by reference to the social contract governing the society in which the competing individuals live—not by reference to any question of identity.

But, all that said, Jane's core identity is affected by the DBS. Does that mean that the DBS cannot be ethically and/or legally justified? The answer is that we do not have the information necessary to say. We do not know (as we knew in Ted's case), the reason for the DBS. There will almost never be an *absolute* prohibition on an interference with identity. That this is so is a consequence of the fact that all individuals are necessarily societal beings—a fact that determines their core identity and also (it is a different point) means that the interests of others will have to be taken into account in deciding whether or not to sanction an identity-affecting intervention.

5.3.3 Anorexia Nervosa

A team of psychiatrists conducted an interview with a patient suffering (and yes, we know both 'patient' and 'suffering' are pejorative words in this context) from Anorexia Nervosa. It went like this:

'*Interviewer: If your anorexia nervosa magically disappeared, what would be different from right now?*
Participant: Everything. My personality would be different.
Interviewer: Really!
Participant: It's been, I know it's been such a big part of me, and—I don't think you can ever get rid of it, or the feelings, you always have a bit—in you [...]
Interviewer: Let's say you've got to this point, and someone said they could wave a magic wand and there wouldn't be anorexia any more.
Participant: I couldn't.
Interviewer: You couldn't.
Participant: It's just part of me now.
Interviewer: Right. So it feels like you'd be losing part of you.
Participant: Because it was my identity.'

CF's answer

There is no avoiding the question of identity here. It follows from our insistence on a relational account of identity that the patient's view of her own identity (and hence of the engagement of identity questions in any treatment decisions) will not be conclusive. But a patient's view of the engagement of their own identity will always be highly material—and so it is here. The relational criterion is also amply satisfied: whatever is done or not done in relation to this patient will have wide and profound repercussive effects on others.

Although the results of the anorexia are objectively horrific (they may lead to the death of the patient—so executing the identity which in other contexts we are so anxious to preserve), we cannot simply say: 'Anorexia is an identity-affecting disease. Medicine exists to cure disease, not to give into it. It is only the pathology that is causing the patient to behave suicidally: cure the pathology and the patient will be herself again—which is the only legitimate aim of medicine.' We must be realistic about prognosis. Assume (as is often the case clinically) that the identity-transforming element of the disease is essentially incurable; that the best result will only ever be remission; that the underlying transmutation of identity is essentially permanent. In those circumstances, respect for the patient's identity must entail adopting, without judgment, the patient's view of herself. There must be no tyranny of the normative or the objective. Who is the patient? It is, in this case, whom she says she is, with the attributes that she identifies.

This conclusion determines some, but not all, of the questions that may arise in relation to the patient's treatment. It makes illegitimate the pathologising of the illness per se because (since there is no clear line between the 'illness' and the patient herself) that would amount to pathologising of the patient herself (a move prohibited by any number of ethical and legal canons). This has the effect of delegitimizing any compulsory treatment of the disease itself. It does not follow, however, that frankly suicidal acts or ideation (*manifestations* of the identity-transforming aspects of the disease, rather than the disease itself) should not be restrained. The justification for this would, again, be based on identity and on prognosis. Self-starvation would kill the identity-bearer, and hence an identity-based analysis will tend to argue against it. If the prognosis in relation to the treatment of the *symptom* of suicidal ideation is good, then compulsory treatment (legally effected under the best interests principle) of that symptom may be justified. It follows from this that if the prognosis in relation to that ideation is sufficiently poor, then (subject to wider, expressivist concerns, broadly based on the need to declare the value of human life) no such compulsion can be justified. This conclusion is, with a few caveats, concordant with the general legal position in England and Wales (*Re E* (*Medical Treatment: Anorexia*) [2012] EWCOP 1639; *Re W* (*Medical Treatment: Anorexia*) [2016] EWCOP 13).

JH's answer

I agree with much of what CF says here. It is interesting that in *Re E* (*Medical Treatment: Anorexia*) [2012] EWCOP 1639, we see the judge seeking to determine whether "the real E" was the current E or the E before the anorexia took hold. I am nervous about CF's suggestion that "respect for the patient's identity must entail adopting, without judgment, the patient's view of herself." I can imagine cases of domestic abuse where a person comes to accept the message of the abuser that they are worthless or that they enjoy being abused. I think the difficulty with anorexia is that our understanding of it is limited. We do not know to what extent it is something like a conversion to a religion or a life-style decision; or to what extent the individual has had an identity imposed upon them (see Hope et al. 2013 for a particularly helpful discussion). Her identity here is as E, with anorexia, but also as E the daughter of her parents, and the friend of those close to her.

5.3.4 Body Dysmorphic Disorder

Barry is 22 years old. He believes that his perfectly normal right leg is grotesquely deformed. He is repeatedly assured that it is not. A diagnosis of Body Dysmorphic Disorder ('BDD') is made. Various psychiatric interventions are tried and fail. In despair, Barry contacts an orthopaedic surgeon and begs him to amputate the leg at the hip.

CF's answer

At first glance it is hard to see any distinction of real ethical or legal weight between this case and the anorexia nervosa case. Yet I consider that there is a distinction. The anorexia affected a root-and-branch change in the patient's identity. It was not simply that she looked at herself in the mirror and considered herself (objectively incorrectly) to be fat. If that were all that the anorexia did, I accept that her case would be indistinguishable from Barry's: a thin body perceived as fat is materially the same as a normal leg seen as deformed. The anorexia patient's malaise (or, more neutrally, re-orientation) was ontological: Barry's is biological and local. There is more to Barry than his right leg; there is little more to the anorexia patient than the self-perception that generates the objectively inaccurate view of herself. The disease has consumed the patient, and when she looks in the mirror she sees the disease and calls it, not inaccurately, herself. Identity does not reside. Identity does not reside in the right leg (although I accept that things that are done or not done to the right leg may, in some circumstances—though not in this—affect identity to an extent that may, on identity grounds, justify surgical intervention).

   That last comment is important. The amputation may very well be justified on grounds that do not engage questions of identity. While we have contended throughout this book that issues of identity are often foundational to the delineation of legal personality (and hence of the rights and duties pertinent to legal personalities), it does not follow that we think that an exhaustive philosophical inquiry into the nature of the identity-issues at stake is always mandatory before a legally or ethically correct decision can be made. Every case will be crucially fact sensitive, but in Barry's case it may well be appropriate to say:

(a) *Whoever* Barry is (and whether or not his identity has been affected by the BDD), he would be better off without the leg.
(b) If he (whoever he is) is truly autonomous, he can validly consent to the removal of the leg.
(c) If he is not autonomous, it is in his best interests for the leg to be removed.

   I appreciate that in many cases in which the best interests jurisdiction it will be necessary to trespass into questions of identity—to ask: *whose* best interests are at stake. But Barry's case may well not be one of them.

JH's answer

I think we need to know much more about Barry's reasons for disliking his leg. We saw in Chap. 4.7 that one of the evils of the continuous negative messages about the appearance of old age is that older people come to dislike their beautifully aging bodies. Similar points are often made about cosmetic surgery on women. The better response in relation to cosmetic surgery may be to challenge the negative message about older people or women's bodies, rather than reinforce those messages by complying with the "autonomy" of the individual. How this plays out in a case of BDD I am not sure. Again, as in the case of anorexia, I suspect we do not know enough about the condition to form a definite view.

5.3.5 Advance Directives

At the age of 50, when she was fit and well, Jean executed an advance directive, compliant with the formalities of the Mental Capacity Act, saying that if she was ever found to have Alzheimer's disease she wanted to forgo all life-sustaining treatment.

She is now 75. Alzheimer's disease was (accurately) diagnosed 2 years ago. She lives in a nursing home, and appears blissfully happy. Before the diagnosis she was a very anxious person. The disease has stripped away a lot of her cerebral cortex, but also all her anxieties. She spends the day watching with huge apparent enjoyment the daytime TV she previously despised, and the evenings laughing and joking with the nurses and the other patients. Everyone who knew her previously comments that there is no apparent continuity between the old Jean and the new Jean. Yes, the body looks the same, but the new Jean seems to retain none of the memories of the old Jean, and certainly has none of the same attitudes or preferences.

Jean gets a chest infection. It would be easy and untraumatic to treat it. The treatment would just be five days of oral antibiotics. But Jean's daughter, who happens to be the sole beneficiary under the will, produces the advance directive and states that it would be an assault if Jean's clinicians gave her the antibiotics.

Jean is plainly incapacitous in the sense that she cannot understand the consequences either of receiving or not receiving the antibiotics. A decision will have to be made for her.

Her doctor proposes to give Jean the medication, saying: 'I have a duty to treat the patient in front of me. That is a patient who plainly wants to live. I owe no duty to a dead woman [the old Jean] who happened to sign a piece of paper twenty five years ago. Why should that piece of paper be a warrant of execution of a woman who didn't exist at the time the document was signed? I wouldn't be justifying in killing, on the instructions of a woman twenty five years ago, a baby born today. Why then should I be complicit in Jean's death?'

CF's answer

As we discussed in Chap. 1, the English law has a philosophically cowardly approach to this sort of problem. It asks simply whether the advance directive is 'valid and applicable' to the relevant situation. That formulation is capable of accommodating an analysis based on the identity of the patient and the identity of the directive-maker (a directive is unlikely to be 'applicable'—a word that gives judges almost infinite scope—if the directive-maker has ceased to be, or has interests wholly different from those of the patient).

We started this book by insisting that wilful or negligent blindness to biological facts is unlikely to lead to good ethical or legal decision-making. That blindness is usually caused by a dogmatic preference for some sort of abstraction over concrete reality. To contend that the old Jean should be the executioner of the new Jean would be a classic illustration of such blindness: the preference there would be for the wholly abstract principle of autonomy (or the equally abstract notion of a Jean who was characterized, to the exclusion of all other considerations, by her personal autonomy) over the obvious interests of the real, new Jean.

I therefore consider that, for both ethical and legal purposes, the old Jean should be acknowledged as having passed away. A new entity, with new rights, obligations and relationships, has come into being. That new entity is the patient for all purposes.

We have repeatedly cautioned against the confusion of identity with attributes, and I can see that it might be said that the personal characteristics of the new Jean are attributes, the significance of which is outweighed by (a) the duration with which other characteristics (those of the old Jean) have existed; and (b) the paramount importance that must be given to clearly expressed autonomous wishes.

I respond really by reiteration: the dead are not entitled to the same as the living. The law's primary concern is for the living. If the dead can be accommodated too, that is all to the good, but where the living and the dead compete, the living must win.

JH's answer

While I agree with much of what CF says here, I think it is just a little too extreme to say the old Jean has "passed away". While I agree that the interests of the new Jean should win out over the claims of the old Jean, it goes too far to say that the old Jean is of no relevance. The case of *Ashan v. University Hospitals Leicester NHS Trust* [2006] *EWHC* 2624 shows the issue well. Ms Ashan had been a devout Muslim who was rendered completely incapacitous as a result of a negligent medical procedure. The question arose whether she should be treated in line with Muslim tradition, or whether she should receive cheaper "standard NHS treatment". The argument was that as she lacked any capacity and would not know how she should be treated she should receive only the standard treatment. Quite rightly the judge rejected this. Although the new Ms Ashan was very different, lacking now the psychological qualities that had been a central part of her identity, these changes had not deprived her of membership of her family or of her religious community. In the same way, Jean is still the "old Jean" in the sense that she is treated as an ongoing member of her family and other relational groups. If she were to die intestate her estate would pass to her family, indicating (that in the eyes of at least that part of the law that deals with inheritance) the new Jean is not completely divorced from the old Jean. None of these points, however, would lead me to disagree with CF's conclusion that we should give Jean the antibiotics she needs.

5.3.6 Permanent Vegetative State

A boy, Terence, is crushed in a crowd. The blood supply to his brain is interrupted. He goes into a Permanent Vegetative State. The diagnosis (which is correctly made) means that he will never again have any capacity for any sensation of any kind. He has no pains and no pleasures. His family sit by his bedside for hours every day for years. He has no idea that they are there. He can breathe unaided. He is fed via a nasogastric tube. Eventually his parents say: 'Enough is enough. Terence really died years ago. What's on the bed is just an empty shell. Stop the feeding.'

CF's answer

It follows from my conclusion in Jean's case that, for essentially the same reasons as we gave there, I agree with Terence's parents: Feeding should be stopped.

My reasons are importantly different from those given by the House of Lords in *Airedale NHS Trust v Bland* [1993] AC 789. The House refused to say that Tony Bland was dead. I think that Terence is. This is because the most fundamental thing about death (far more fundamental than the cessation of breathing or the cessation of electrical activity in the brain stem) is the ablation of identity. I therefore propose a new definition of death for all medico-legal purposes: *the irretrievable loss of any sort of identity.* The words 'any sort' are important. They mean, for instance, that one could not pronounce death in the case of the new Jean: the old Jean and the new Jean share a body; the old Jean's identity has died (has been irretrievably lost—except in the sense that it lives on in the memories of others), but the new Jean has a clear identity. One could not kill the body jointly owned by the old Jean without killing the new Jean—which would be wrong.

In Terence's case, everything that made him him has been lost. This might sound like a manichaestic denigration of the body: it is not. I simply say that bodies without the other identity-defining elements are not really proper bodies. Bodies are intended to move to the bidding of whatever it is that constitutes the identity: the self. In old-fashioned (but rather compelling) language: the soul is the reason for the body, not the body for the soul.

JH's answer

I agree with much of what CF has said, but would place greater weight on the view of Terence's parents. As argued in Chap. 4, caring relationships generate considerable moral value. While Terence's parents had been interacting with and engaging with Terence there was a relationship to treasure. Once they decided it was finished, there was nothing of value that the law needs to protect.

5.3.7 Criminal Liability and Temporary Aberration: Self-induced Intoxication

Jonathan is a gentle, considerate, loving teetotaler. One night, saddened by his book sales, he drinks a bottle of whisky. He becomes enraged, and strangles his wife. In the morning, when he sees what he has done (and although he has no memory at all of the events of the previous night) he is consumed with remorse, and resolves to spend his life trying to atone. He is arrested, charged with murder, and finally convicted or manslaughter on the grounds of diminished responsibility. The psychiatric reports indicate that there is no possibility at all of any repetition of comparable behavior.

Our answer

Ethics and law diverge. The real Jonathan is easy enough to identify. He is the gentle family man. Ethically his fault is drinking a bottle of whisky; not homicide. Legally, his case is a powerful illustration of the need to abolish the anachronistic distinction between murder and manslaughter and have instead a crime of homicide of varying degrees of culpability. The law (for metaphysically uninteresting reasons concerned with the declaration of the value of human lives, and *pour encourager les autres*) should punish the body that did the strangling, notwithstanding that that body was and is and will be wholly unconnected with any identity that continues to exist and can itself be the subject of punishment. This is one example of a case where the law is entirely correct to ignore the question of identity (although Jonathan's past and future identity and its lack of connection with the crime will of course be relevant to sentence/'his' place on the hierarchy of homicide offences). Jonathan's crime should fall towards the bottom of that hierarchy.

5.3.8 Criminal Liability: Dissociative Identity Disorder

James suffers from a condition known as Dissociative Identity Disorder ('DID'), in which several personas appear to cohabit. While one of them (whom we will call Hyde) is dominant, James (if it is indeed him) goes onto the street and bludgeons a passer-by to death. By the time that James is arrested, Hyde has regressed, and has been replaced by the eminently respectable Jekyll. The medical evidence is that Hyde can be pharmacologically killed. James, who has no idea where Hyde was or what Hyde was doing, happily agrees to the death of Hyde.

Our answer

In Chap. 1 we expressed our misgivings about the assumptions made by this case about the nature of DID. For the purposes of this consideration we put those misgivings to one side and assume that Hyde and Jekyll have discrete identities (in the sense that we have been talking about identity until now).

If this assumption is correct, then our newly promulgated definition of death (see Terence's case above) creates a difficulty: it would mean that the person who administered the drug that 'kills' Hyde would be guilty of murder.

Having gone this far, we cannot shrink from that conclusion: yes, it is prima facie murder. But there is a defence: self-defence/the defence of others. If Hyde is allowed to roam free (and there is no indication that he can be subdued other than by death), people will die on the street. More interestingly, Jekyll will be damaged too: Jekyll's body will be arrested and incarcerated or, in some jurisdictions, killed. All of those things will affect the expression of Jekyll's identity to such a degree that to kill Hyde cannot be said to be disproportionate.

Legally and ethically, then, Hyde should be killed.

5.3.9 Suicidal Ideation

Kate is severely depressed. She makes a bolt for the edge of a cliff, but is rugby-tackled by Dave, sectioned, and admitted to a mental hospital. Her depression is treated. Several months later she writes a letter to Dave, thanking him for 'saving' 'her', and saying that at the time she was 'not in [her] right mind.'

Our answer

We are nervous in approaching this question, because we realize that states at least akin to depression might be regarded as integral parts of the normal human condition, or at least as an integral part of the weave of some individuals. But as, so often, the question turns on its own facts. Kate does not appear to be a constitutionally depressed person—or if she is, the profound depression that propelled her towards the cliff edge seems to be so far from her baseline that it cannot be said to be part of her. If that's right, we have alighted on another interesting fact about identity: that the core identity is more like a bell curve than a parcel: a characteristic of a *sort* that might belong in some quantities within the curve (and would in those quantities be essentially constitutive of self) will, if too abundant, be incapable of being accommodated within the curve. Then you get pathology: and it is likely to be an identity-eroding kind of pathology.

So in Kate's case there is neither an ethical nor a legal difficulty. The tackle and the compulsory admission and treatment can all be justified ethically as identity-preserving. If Kate had gone over the cliff there would have been no identity left to preserve. Any doubt about the ethics of preventing her (possibly genuinely autonomous) suicide should, the precautionary principle suggests, be resolved in favour of maintaining the status quo: and that means the tackle.

The law's approach is broadly similar, although it is more coy about using the language of identity. Its concern, under the Mental Health Act, is to treat the underlying disease and hence to restore normality: it assumes that normality is an absence of pathology, and that normality in this sense is desirable. Those assumptions can be questioned: indeed we have questioned them ourselves (Foster and Herring 2014). But on the facts of Kate's case they do not need to be inter-rogated. The Act seeks to mitigate the consequence of an identity-eroding disease: the Act is the guardian of identity.

5.3.10 Schizophrenia

'I am my brother', asserts Ken, who has been diagnosed with schizophrenia.

Our answer

We need more facts. But we would note, as for the Jekyll and Hyde case, that cohabitation in one body of more than one identity is rarely placid. There is usually room only for one identity. Where cohabitation produces strife, it will often (as in the Jekyll and Hyde case) be easy enough to justify ethically (without any gym-nastics) and legally (using our notion of identity-death and some sort of rescue principle), the selection reduction of one identity in order to save the other. This case, though, is different from the DID case: it is not a straightforward instance of cohabitation. Ken insists not that his brother shares his space, but that he *is* his brother. It is no different in principle from the conventional schizophrenic who believes that he is John the Baptist.

Here we can see no justification for intervention—except in the event of the apparently wrong identity creating some sort of danger to others. The normative should not tyrannise except in the interests of public health or morals. We really have no idea whether Ken is his brother, or even what the statement means. Identity is mysterious enough: for all we know Ken might be expounding impressively one corner of the mystery.

5.3.11 Dyslexia

A 7 year old boy, Jim, is diagnosed with dyslexia.

'It's a good job we caught it early', said his teacher. 'We'll be able to cure it, more or less. There are all sorts of strategies we can use these days. He'll be near normal by the time we've finished with him.' His parents are horrified.

Our answer

The parents are right to be horrified. Jim's dyslexic's view of the world cannot be prised apart from his identity. If it were possible to cure his dyslexia, that would be tantamount to an execution of Jim. We doubt that such a cure is or ever will be possible, but well-meaning therapeutic efforts might leave the patient dead on the table. Ethically such efforts, because of the risk they pose, cannot be justified. Legally they are applauded by many, because of the pathologizing of dyslexia, the worship of the normative, and the unquestioned priority given to the left brain. Adoption of our identity-definition of death would mean that such efforts would lead to a finding of murder or manslaughter if the efforts were successful, or a finding of causing grievous bodily harm with or without intent.

   This case highlights the issue of authenticity, and illustrates the relationship between authenticity and identity. The well-meaning would-be educators are trying to make Jim inauthentic: something other than himself. If the inauthenticity goes to an identity-defining trait (as we have suggested is the case here), and is persisted in long enough to produce indelible changes, it will be identity-modifying. Not all inauthentic acts will have this effect: most of them will relate to identity-traits, but most will be insufficiently effective in causing permanent change to meet the criteria. Education of course does produce permanent physical changes: that's its whole point. A teacher's job is to facilitate neuronal connections—changes just as physical as a bruise from corporal punishment. We suggest that the only legitimate education is education that allows someone to be more fully themselves (a formulation that betrays our assumptions about that essential but vulnerable core self): the re-educative boot camp proposed for Jim does not do that.

5.3.12 An Out of Body Experience

Andy dislocates his shoulder. He goes to the Casualty department of the local hospital, where an attempt is made to relocate it under 'gas and air' (nitrous oxide and air: commonly used for analgesia during childbirth). While this is being done he experiences an 'Out of Body Experience' (commonly abbreviated to 'OBE") in which 'he' seems to float out of his body and look down on it. 'He' can see the clinicians' efforts to put the shoulder back in place, and 'he' is conscious of the intense pain in the shoulder, but he has a curious detachment from this pain: it does not seem to be entirely 'his'. Eventually he passes out. When he comes to, he is his normal self, not aware of any division between his body and any other part of him. The clinicians have, however, not managed to relocate the shoulder.

Our answer

This dramatic example takes us back to reiterate and cautiously endorse (at least as a rough rule of thumb for the purposes of practical law and ethics) the popular, intuitive view of identity with which the book started: the view that insists that there is indeed a core identity, distinct from the body, directing the body's conscious actions, but dependent on the body for expression and accommodation. This, we note with something like embarrassment, is the academically unfashionable Cartesian dualism. We are well aware of the attacks on this very basic form of dualism that have been made by modern neuroscience. One of us has considered those arguments in detail elsewhere (Foster 2012). Anyone convinced by the arguments of mainstream neuroscience (which do not consider seriously or at all experiences like Andy's) will cite back at us our insistence that one should start ethical and legal deliberations by getting the biological facts right, and that since the biological facts are on their side, anything ethical or legal that we seek to build on the foundation of Cartesian dualism is built on the sand. We have, then, a disagreement about the foundational facts which we cannot resolve between the covers of this book.

But even if we have misconstrued the neuroscience, we think that we still have a defence. For inalienable intuitions (such as the dualist intuition) *are facts*—and arguably more significant facts (because we can never displace them) in the context of ethical and legal decision-making than more merely chemical facts. If we try to construct counter-intuitive ethics or law that will get us into a far greater mess than if we try to construct a counter-physiological system.

5.3.13 *Midazolam and Memory*

Since the clinicians have not managed to sort out Andy's dislocated shoulder using gas and air as analgesia, they have to try something else. They give him a dose of midazolam. This is a sedative but also, importantly, an amnesiac. While Andy is under its influence he can plainly feel pain: he winces and cries out, but can hear and respond obediently to the doctors' instructions. The procedure is successful. When the drug wears off, Andy has absolutely no recollection whatever of the doctors' attempts. The last thing he remembers was the anaesthetist saying that she was about to administer the midazolam.

Our answer

This, together with Oliver Sacks' case of Jimmy the submariner, illustrates that the distinction between attributes and identity, which we have insisted is fundamental, is, like so much else in this debate, a matter of fact and degree. Memory is certainly an attribute, but if sufficient of the attribute is lost, identity may be changed or eroded. Nobody would say that Andy's loss of an hour affected his identity: few would say that Jimmie, stuck prior to 1975, is not a materially different person from a Jimmie not so affected by Korsakov's syndrome, and that the material differences entail, or are constituted by, a difference in identity. We have implicitly indicated, in our responses to the other cases, how we would react to various legal or ethical conundrums relating to identity-altering memory loss.

5.4   Conclusion

We hope that, if it has achieved nothing else, this book has highlighted the significance of personhood and autonomy for some of the key debates in law and
ethics. We do not purport to have answered all the questions raised. Indeed, as is
apparent in this chapter, we do not agree between ourselves about the answer in
every case. What we have illustrated is that the simple answer that the self is merely
a biological or psychological entity is misconceived. Our moral value (our personhood) and our identities are a complex mix of biology, psychology and
relationship. Our aim is to start a discussion on this overlooked issue, which is of
considerable significance to lawyers and ethicists.

References

Foster C (2012) Wired for God?. The Biology of Spiritual Experience Hodder, London
Foster C, Herring J (2014) What is health? In: Freeman M (ed) Law and global health. Oxford
    University Press, Oxford
Hope T, Tan J, Stewart A, McMillan J (2013) 'Agency, ambivalence and authenticity: the many
    ways in which anorexia nervosa can affect autonomy'. Intl J Law Context 9:20–36
Ware K (1979) The orthodox way. Mowbray, London